Experience *Real* Satisfaction

How Life at The Fountain Satisfies the Longings of Our Soul

—Sarah Goebel—

On Assignment
PUBLISHING
Our Assignment is to Help You Complete Yours

On Assignment Publishing
Ridgecrest, CA 93555
www.onassignmentpublishing.com

Previous Edition published in 2010

Experience REAL Satisfaction
Revised edition includes Study Guide Answers & Leader's Guide

Printed in the United States of America

ISBN: 978-0-9842428-9-4

On Assignment Publishing books are available in bookstores everywhere, and on the Web at www.Amazon.com

Endorsements

"Sarah presents strong biblical guidance to lead you to GENUINE SATISFACTION starting right where you are and with what you have. Every woman needs the principles of this book written on her heart."

–Gloria Cotten
President, Wellspring Int'l Women's Ministries

"This book will take you on a journey that will give guidance in the desperate place. It is a journey that will take you into the place of His presence, and ultimately to the place called Satisfaction. This book is filled with Scripture, hope and joy. I am sure all who read it will find Satisfaction!"

–Wayne Tate
Worship Pastor Manna Church, Fayetteville, NC

"Sarah's unique mix of personal transparency, scriptural insight, and excellent communication skills combine to make this book a valuable resource for anyone seeking true satisfaction. The format of the book suits it perfectly for either small group studies or personal devotionals. The content of the book is rich, and you will find studying it time well spent."

–Jennifer Kennedy Dean
Executive Director, The Praying Life Foundation
Author of best-selling Live a Praying Life

"Sarah lays out KEY PRINCIPLES every Christian should know in order to live a genuinely fulfilled, satisfied life. This is a recommended read!!!"

–Michael Fletcher, Sr.
Pastor, Manna Church Fayetteville, NC

Dedications

*F*irst, I dedicate this book to my mother who went home to be with our Lord on September 30, 2006. Thank you, Mom, for your love, encouragement and example of perseverance.

Secondly, I dedicate this book to my two children who were born of my flesh. Ginger, I am so proud of the caring and faithful woman you have become. Jason, I am equally as proud of the responsible and caring man you are today. Thank you both for your love and friendship. I thank God for you and I praise Him that you are not only my children, but also my sister and brother in Christ.

Thirdly, I dedicate this book to all those who will persevere the necessary process of change, enduring the journey to receive the prize that lies at the end of it. May you always live your lives by faith; be fulfilled and satisfied; and may your lives glorify God the Father and the Lord Jesus Christ!

Appreciations

I give thanks to my patient, unselfish and loyal husband, Jon, who always loves me and encourages me in all that the Lord sets before me. Thank you, Jon, for not allowing me to quit on the dreams that God has placed in my heart. When God brought you into my life, He redeemed and restored all that had been lost and broken.

And above all, I thank my Lord Jesus Christ for loving me, saving me, enabling me, comforting me and encouraging me, to bring me "to such a time as this." Thank you Lord for allowing me to be a part of what You are doing on the earth. To You, Lord Jesus, be the glory forever!

Table of Contents

Introduction ────────────────────────

Satisfying the Restless Soul
────────────────────────

*Then I applied myself to the understanding of
wisdom, and also of madness and folly, but I learned
that this, too, is a chasing after the wind.*

Ecclesiastes 1:17

*J*esus said, *The thief comes only in order to steal and kill and destroy. I came that they may have and enjoy life, and have it in abundance (to the full, till it overflows)* (John 10:10 AMP). I ask you – Are you enjoying your life? Are you enjoying it in abundance? Because if you are a Christian, Jesus said He came and walked the earth, died and resurrected so that you could have an abundant and satisfied life.

Yet, many Christians are singing the song, "I can't get no satisfaction. I try and I try… but I just can't find it." Truly, the desire for satisfaction seems greater today than ever before. I have witnessed myself along with others, from across the financial spectrum of society, every denomination and age, all searching for what seems to be elusive – a life experiencing lasting peace, joy and satisfaction. There is dissatisfaction with our jobs, ministries, health, finances, and circumstances, people who are in our lives, material goods, ourselves and God. We are not happy with who we are or what our station in life is. Yet, Jesus said He came to give us a whole and satisfied life. Therefore, I found myself asking, how is it so many in the church are dissatisfied?

God tells us in Hosea 4:6 that His people are destroyed for lack of knowledge. Could this be the reason for our lack of contentment? Wishing to avoid destruction myself and hoping to access the abundance of John 10:10, I went on a quest to gain knowledge, desiring most to learn how to be content and satisfied with life and help others to do the same. In this book, I share my experiences, and lessons learned from counseling others in their dissatisfaction, while considering my own disappointments, hearkening to the Holy Spirit, and searching the Word of God on this matter. I pray my findings will help you get off the merry-go-round of disappointment and onto the road leading to genuine contentment. I also hope this book becomes a tool or resource you can use to help someone you may know who has a restless soul, longing for something more.

This book is an interactive personal or group study. Each chapter ends with one or more highlighted insights designed to move you forward in your journey. I have included Scriptures for memorization and several questions at the end of each chapter for your reflection, designed to help with the application of what you have studied. To receive the most from this biblical principled study, you should take the time to read, reflect and answer these questions personally. If you are participating in a group study, choose a few of these questions to discuss together. Also included is a short prayer to help you communicate with God concerning the material you review, whether alone or as a group. In addition, a brief leader's guide is found in the back of the book.

Through this study, I pray you will gain an understanding of how God Himself imparts satisfaction into our lives and what your role in this process is. You will learn to identify dissatisfaction, learn the dangers of it, gain an understanding of what true satisfaction is, recognize its benefits, learn why we wrestle with dissatisfaction, and learn how to experience satisfaction on a sustained basis.

Progress requires that you determine to honestly examine your own heart. In this way, unproductive and unscriptural habits and attitudes will be identified and replaced with new ones so you can enjoy the benefits of living a satisfied life. You will need to ask yourself, *Am I truly satisfied?* If not, ask: In what areas of my life am I discontent? What are the reasons for my discontentment? Do I get upset when things are not going my way? Am I angry towards God or in unforgiveness towards another? Could it be that I want the life God has given someone else instead of the life He has given me? Do I think I am so special I should be void of problems and challenges that others in the world face? Be honest in your examination, with yourself and with God, as you use these questions to bring light to what is going on deep within your heart. God already knows every thought and feeling that is tucked away in the crevices of your heart, but it is only by sharing openly with God that you will find genuine, lasting satisfaction.

As your blessings grow because of increased satisfaction, it is my hope you will be a witness so others, too, will learn and experience the benefits of a contented life. In prayer, I now release the pages of this book as an eternal deposit from my life to yours.

With Love & for Christ's glory,

Sarah

Chapter 1————————————————————

Dreaming Dreams – *Is it All Vanity?*

Everything is meaningless. What does man gain from
all his labor at which he toils under the sun?
Ecclesiastes 1:3

*D*efinitions for the word dream found in *The American Heritage College Dictionary* include: "a wild fancy or hope; or a condition or achievement that is longed for; an aspiration."[1] So, let's take an assessment. What is it that you are longing for? What dreams are you dreaming?

You may dream about great success in position and wealth. If you are single, you may fantasize about getting married. And if you are married, you may dream of being single again. Perhaps your dream is a new car. Or you may be a woman who thinks a name-brand wardrobe is the missing link to your satisfaction. Some have thought that having a baby would be the event that would surely result in sustained joy, happiness and satisfaction. How about you golfers? ..... If you are a golfer like my husband, you may think scoring a 68 every round would change your life. Of course, it might change it. You could potentially end up on the pro circuit. However, it is not the ingredient needed for a satisfied, happy life. In fact, you could find yourself feeling even more dissatisfied as it just might create new issues in your days. This is often true with many of our dreams. We are unable to see the problems that the changes we dream of could result in. Besides, most of us have found that when our wishes become reality, there is another complaint, another need in which its fulfillment is seen as the remedy to the dissatisfaction of our restless souls.

Get honest with yourself. Do you toil in your work whether at home, the office or church even to the point of exhaustion, yet never experience fulfillment? Or perhaps you regret your choices or failures of the past. Are you saying *if only?* If only I had not done this or that or had done it... If only I had been or could be... If only I could just have this or just do that... then, I would be content. Are you feeling as though life is empty and futile, thinking nothing will bring any lasting fulfillment, as did Matthew Arnold in his poem "Rugby Chapel"?

> Most men eddy about
> Here and there—eat and drink, Chatter
> and love and hate, Gather and squander,
> are raised Aloft, are hurl'd in the dust,
> Striving blindly, achieving
> Nothing; and then they die—[2]

I can relate to this poem. I remember a season in my life when I was living continually on a merry-go-round in search for satisfaction, restless and going nowhere. How about you? Do you relate to the feelings expressed in this poem? Many do, or have, including people we have studied in the Bible.

Take King Solomon for example. He had everything – wisdom, power and riches. If ever there was a person to live who had all the resources needed to explore and search out the meaning of life, it was he. After devoting himself to study and exploration of all that is done on earth, he concluded in the first part of his journey that everything done in life is meaningless. He compared our attempt to satisfy ourselves to trying to quench the thirst of the desert sand. We can guess he found no satisfaction with his findings at this point in his journey.

It is interesting to note that "Solomon was looking at a society that was similar to today's society. There were injustices to the poor; crooked politics, incompetent leaders, guilty people allowed to continue to commit more crime, materialism, and a desire for 'the good old days.'"[3] It doesn't sound like the world has changed much, does it? Solomon wrote under the inspiration of the Holy Spirit; yet, he was not writing from a heavenly perspective. He wrote from a human point of view applying human reasoning to the complexities and problems of life. Viewing life from a human perspective, instead of considering God's presence and power, purpose and plan, in the midst of life, always results in a negative summation.

I have heard many people say that if they could win the lottery, they would be satisfied. Many in the world cheat, steal and kill for money. But King Solomon with all his wealth, power and position proclaimed there was no contentment or meaning to life. He realized the insatiable nature of man, that there is no satisfaction in riches or any of life's pursuits. One would always want more.

Proverbs 30:15-16 says:
Greed as twins, each named "Give me!"
There are three or four things that are never satisfied:
The world of the dead and a childless wife, the thirsty
earth and a flaming fire.

The Message Bible says the twins are named *"Gimme"* and *"Gimme more"* (30:15 MSG). No matter how rich you are...no matter what rewards you have received or goals conquered. . . no matter how many blessings God has poured out on your life (He does bless the unjust as well as the just) ...without Christ, you will still covet more and you will never be satisfied.

1 Timothy 6:10 (CEV):
The love of money causes all kinds of trouble. Some
people want money so much that they have given up their
faith and caused themselves a lot of pain.

This Scripture says that some begin to put their faith in their money, instead of God, and it causes them trouble. On the other hand, is it wrong for Christians to have wealth and enjoy their lives? Is it wrong to dream dreams? Absolutely not! Desires motivate us to set goals. Goals accomplished, change lives. The problem is not desires in themselves, but what kind of desires it is that are consuming us. The key is living life in such a way that our desires are godly ones. In other words, we need to seek the Kingdom of God first and allow God to give us His desires. We should ask God to line our hearts up with His. Psalm 37:4 teaches us God will not only put His desires in our hearts, but he will also fulfill them in our lives. How awesome! Yet, so many times we allow the world to shape the desires of our hearts resulting in a chase of the wind, a life without fulfillment. God has so much more for us. In fact, Scripture tells us that those, who belong to God, have available to them wealth, and pleasure.

> 1 Timothy 6:17:
> *Command those who are rich in this present world not to be arrogant nor to put their hope in wealth, which is so uncertain, but to put their hope in God, who richly provides us with everything for our enjoyment.*

As we put our hope in God, He richly gives us everything and He gives it for a purpose – He gives it for the purpose of our enjoyment!

Wealth can be here today and gone tomorrow; therefore, it is foolish to put our hope in it. Whereas, when our hope is in God, He provides and even restores what is sometimes lost. He is unchangeable and He is a giving God. Consider the story of Job – his great losses and how God restored two times over. This knowledge of God, coupled with a relationship with Christ, enables us to maintain our satisfaction in our times of loss and grieving the death of our dreams.

Again, it is imperative to surrender our desires and allow God's dreams to become our own. This happens when we commune with Him. These God-given visions will produce the fruit of satisfaction; whereas, desires that are not from God flow from our fallen nature which produces selfish and evil fancies. When they are fulfilled, we are left empty and frustrated. Jeremiah 10:23 says: *I know, O LORD, that a man's life is not his own; it is not for man to direct his steps.* If we do not put God first in our lives, keeping Him as our Fountain of Living Waters, allowing His Lordship over our hearts, then our desires will flow from an evil heart. We effectually jump back onto that merry-go-round, walking in circles in search of satisfaction. Lusting, coveting, desiring something that God has not given to us only results in dissatisfaction. We need to keep Matthew 6:33 before us at all times, and act on it: *Seek first the Kingdom of God and His righteousness and He will add all of these things to you.* God is faithful to give us godly desires and to direct our steps to fulfill them if we will keep Him number one in our lives. On the other hand, self-directed steps lead to dissatisfaction.

Dissatisfaction can lead one down the path of deception. Think about the account of Eve in the Garden of Eden. The devil planted seeds of dissatisfaction into her heart by entering her thoughts. He tempted her to believe the lie that God was withholding something from her – knowledge— which when she contemplated this lie, resulted in her disobeying God. A desire for that which God had not given her – the knowledge she would find by eating from the Tree of Knowledge of Good & Evil – was cultivated as a result of her contemplating the lie told her. Then, un-godly desire led to disobedience (an un-godly desire is any desire that is not deposited by God). She became dissatisfied and wanted more, even though everything God had created was at her disposal except for this one thing. Her dissatisfaction led to the fall of man and his separation from God. How serious discontentment can be!

Dissatisfaction, if not kept in check, can be dangerous. It can lead to great devastation in our personal lives and the lives of our children, grandchildren and other descendants (See Deuteronomy 28). We must avoid discontentment from ruling our lives by walking in obedience to God and keeping our eyes on Him. We need to control our thoughts and guard our hearts by cultivating a heart of gratitude. We can begin by focusing on those things we have to be thankful for, starting with the gift of eternal salvation. Most of us can find many things to thank God for. As you praise God for the good in your life, dissatisfaction will begin to turn to joy.

Without God's influence, dreaming dreams and desiring things we shouldn't is inevitable for two glaring reasons. First, since the fall of man, the world and all within it, including humankind, have been tainted by sin. Romans 8:19-21 tells us the result is the confusion of creation as it waits expectantly for the son of God to be revealed.

This confusion is seen in the lives of humans as they live out their lives in deception and the sin of idolatry. Humans are deceived with dreams for all the wrong things, believing they can find satisfaction in having more money, possessions, friends and attention. Yet, John 4:14 points out: Christ is the only true source of living water. He is our source of satisfaction – a source of unending supply. After all, God is unchangeable; whereas, circumstances, people, positions and things are imperfect and sure to change. Therefore, if we count on any of these for a satisfied life, our satisfaction will be fleeting. It will come and go like the morning dew on the spring grass. Things in the world – husbands, wives, friendships, promotions, awards, entertainment, pleasures, material possessions and money can bring us a level of happiness and enjoyment. They can make our lives easier, but they cannot bring sustained satisfaction that brings peace to our soul.

"The truth is God Himself planted a longing in our soul to be healed of the wounded spirit rent in the human race when we rebelled and pulled away from Him. It is the longing to be whole again."[4] The reality is this: "God has sculpted us humans for eternity (Ecc 3:11), and the crumbs of time fail to satisfy our undying souls."[5] This void is intended to cause us to seek after God but instead we walk around with feelings of discontentment gnawing away at our satisfaction as we run to one thing and another searching for fulfillment. We could instead run to God and find satisfaction and delight. Psalm 36:8-9 reveals: *They feast on the abundance of your house; you give them drink from your river of delights. For with you is the fountain of life; in your light we see light.*

In Ecclesiastes 12:1-8 we discover that Solomon eventually found the answer to his dilemma regarding life's meaning and fulfillment. God changed his heart and he found the contentment he was looking for. He concluded that without God, all truly is vanity. On the other hand, a life lived for God has meaning and satisfaction. This life will find purpose and fulfillment. Christ living through us and us living in Christ is the true abundant life!

So you can see, Christians are not left to restless and dissatisfied hearts. If you have begun a relationship with God in Christ, you have the opportunity to live your life centered on God in communion with Him. You have hope to quench any and all insatiable desires that rise up because you have this God-centered hope through Jesus Christ. Praise the Lord, there is more to our lives than what we see in this physical world.

Christ is the One who gives us the ability to do what we do; He is the source for all that we have. He is our source for dreams that when fulfilled bring a sense of fulfillment and joy. He is our source for satisfaction. But, to experience Christ, as such, requires that we live intentionally for Christ through cultivating a deep relationship beyond our salvation. It requires effort, as does personal satisfaction, because it requires a pursuit of God. Satisfaction does not come without a conscious pursuit and it does not come naturally. And, it is only available to believers due to their faith relationship with Jesus Christ.

If you are restless, disgruntled and unhappy, yearning for that thing that you don't have and possibly can't have, making a decision today to put the effort forth to pursue more of God is your first step toward satisfaction. Paul says in Philippians 4:11 that he learned to be content no matter what his circumstances were. It didn't matter if he was abased or abounding, he was satisfied in the place God had him. He learned satisfaction through his relationship with Christ as it was experienced in the circumstances of His life. This should be encouraging to us. If Paul learned this, so can we. Like Paul's, our journey to contentment is an experiential progression of satisfaction learned through the situations of life. We can have it if we will determine to spend time with Christ as Paul did. The question is, will we? We will if we want it bad enough. In Philippians 4:10-13 we find a glimpse of Paul's journey to satisfaction to include:

- He learned to draw on God's strength and power.
- He learned to view life from above – from God's perspective
- He learned to focus and hold fast the promises of God

It is good to know that we are not doomed to the to-be-pitied life of dissatisfaction. As Christians, we can follow Paul's example. We can have a positive hopeful attitude towards life, no matter what. We do have hope by the grace of God for His impartation and teaching in contentment. But there is even more good news. As stated in the introduction, John 10:10 tells us Jesus came to make available to us life and life *abundant!* This Greek word "Perissos" is used here, indicating that God is here to take us into "a superabundant, excessive, overflowing, surplus, over and above, more than enough, profuse, extraordinary, above the ordinary, more than sufficient kind of life."[6] Because Christ is more than enough for any situation, we can be satisfied through our relationship with Him.

However, Christ's idea of the abundant life may be quite different than some. Although God does take care of our needs, I believe Christ's focus is on the attitudes of the heart and how those attitudes can result in satisfaction, joy and peace, regardless of circumstances. He set us free from the bondage of sin and empowers us to choose what is right. We have been enabled to take control of our thoughts, emotions and attitudes. His grace is sufficient and will empower us for any situation we may encounter. Christ has made available *healing* for our wounded hearts, minds and bodies and *reconciliation* to our Creator God who is the only true source for living a satisfied life. This is the abundant life! Our life lived in Christ! Our meaning, purpose and fulfillment are found in Him.

Beware not to confuse satisfaction with complacency. Contentment is experienced by those who are practicing the actions of 2 Peter 1:5-9: *add to your faith goodness; and to goodness, knowledge; and to knowledge, self-control; and to self-control, perseverance; and to perseverance, godliness; and to godliness, mutual affection; and to mutual affection, love.* It doesn't happen without effort. In contrast, complacency is passive. It looks kind of religious – a quiet life void of any dreams. We know that is not of God. As we have already discussed, God wants us to have dreams and desires. He just wants them to be imparted by Him. And He loves to impart dreams bigger than ourselves. These are the dreams we will depend on Him to fulfill.

The complacent Christians are sometimes those who have walked with the Lord for a number of years and have lost their passion for Christian living as Christ has called us to live it. The things of God have become so familiar; they now take them for granted and they have quit doing anything to move forward with the Lord and His plan. Christians who have been hurt by misled leadership in the church sometimes lose their passion for Christian service as well. Others fall into complacency as they become distracted by problems or worldly pleasures. Complacency is dangerous as it leads to dissatisfaction and a life of idolatry. Christians need to ask God to stir up a hunger within their soul to know more of Him. God is so awesome that we can never know everything there is about Him. It's impossible to experience Him in all of His fullness. We can, however, dig deeper in the Word of God and find treasure there that will spur us on to deeper intimacy. We can pray for dreams and passion to be reignited in our hearts for God and His desires. I hope you will look around you and begin to discern His presence in your life. Be faithful to the spiritual disciplines of prayer, meditation, bible study and praise. He will meet you where you are and begin to reveal more of Himself to you. He is waiting for you.

God wants to place desires on our hearts and then fulfill them. *Delight yourself in the LORD; And He will give you the desires of your heart. Commit your way to the LORD, Trust also in Him, and He will do it* (Psalm 37:4-5). This tells me that progress is important to God. Contentment is active and is not found in complacency. Yet, it is important to understand that we are to be thankful and content where God has us at the present, while He is working through us to fulfill our goals. Be content where you are while on the way to where you are going.

I believe in setting goals for every area of life: body, soul (mind, will, emotions) and spirit. We should have spiritual, physical and knowledge goals that have been born out of our time spent with God. Goals help us measure progress and God has created us in such a way that we are more satisfied when we are progressing toward the goals He has given us.

Living for Christ gives our life purpose and meaning that no one and no circumstance can take away. Living with purpose brings contentment to our inner being; and as we live in Christ, He gives us desires that effect eternity.

A relationship with God where genuine satisfaction flows freely begins with the acceptance of Jesus Christ as your Savior and Lord. This Jesus Christ of Nazareth, came from heaven as a man born of a virgin; lived a righteous life, then took our place on the cross and died for the punishment of our sins as payment for our sins. He was then resurrected to life that we who receive His gift of salvation may be forgiven, reconciled to God and live forever with God.

If you don't know Jesus Christ, then it is true that "all is vanity" because everything you do, everything you have, and everything you are, will one day perish. But, if you belong to Christ, you have the opportunity to invest in that which is eternal, and as you do, you find yourself genuinely satisfied today and for all eternity. However, if you have not yet received

Jesus Christ as your Lord and Savior, you will be continually searching to fill the void in your soul.

If you grew up in church or if you consider yourself to be a Christian, yet you find that you are always anxious and dissatisfied; or, if you are not absolutely sure of your salvation, living with doubt that if you were to die today you would be with God forever, then I recommend you take this time to confirm your salvation. You need to know for sure that you have eternal life with God. Before we continue on our journey, I want to encourage you to take a couple of minutes to see what the Bible says about eternal life. Please turn to Appendix A to discover how to enter into an eternal relationship with Christ.

Moments at the Fountain

Reflection & Application

Things to Remember

- Life's meaning & purpose is found in Christ's life lived through ours as we walk out our relationship in Him.

- Contentment is learned in surrender to Christ where we exchange our desires for His and He brings them to fruition.

- Viewing life from God's vantage point, and holding fast to His promises, results in power for satisfied living.

Philippians 4:11-13 (NASB)
...for I have learned to be content in whatever circumstances I am. I know how to get along with humble means, and I also know how to live in prosperity; in any and every circumstance I have learned the secret of being filled and going hungry, both of having abundance and suffering need. I can do all things through Him who strengthens me.

John 10:10
The thief comes only to steal and kill and destroy; I have come that they may have life, and have it to the full.

Ecclesiastes 1:3

> *What do people gain from all their labors*
> *at which they toil under the sun?*
> *Generations come and generations go,*
> *but the earth remains forever.*

Psalm 37:4

> *Take delight in the LORD, and he will give you the desires of*
> *your heart.*

Reflect & Grow

1. Consider the various areas of your life, i.e. marriage, singleness, parenting, family heritage, job, church life, physical life, social life, spiritual life. Do you find yourself dissatisfied on a regular basis in any of them? What areas do you regularly say life is too busy, too hard, too painful or too boring? What can you change to eliminate this kind of discontentment? Consider what you could change in your thinking? Consider what you can change in your actions. Consider the things that are unchangeable and ask God to help you accept those.

2. Do you think Solomon's society had similarities to today's society? Has the world changed much? If we view life from the same perspective as did Solomon, what might we conclude about our lives today? What perspective should we approach life by, if we are to find contentment?

3. Is it possible to be satisfied in a present circumstance while having a goal that when reached will change our situation?

4. What are some of the situations in the New Testament that the Apostle Paul found himself in, though he declares in every situation (whether abased or abounding), he had learned to be content (Philippians 4:11-13)? Read Philippians 1:18-22. What was it about his life, which is so different than most, that enabled him to experience this kind of supernatural satisfaction?

5. Read Psalm 90:14. What does the psalmist ask for? What does he say it will result in? Turn this psalm into a prayer for your life over the next twelve weeks.

6. Remember the contrasted conclusions of Solomon in the first half of the Book of Ecclesiastes and chapter twelve of the same book. When is all in life vanity? When is it not?

7. Consider the difference between complacency and contentment in the body of Christ. Then read 2 Peter 1:12-14. What do we need to do on a regular basis to stir up a desire within that will motivate us to pursue more of God?

8. What is meant by viewing things from above the sun, versus viewing them from below it? Are there any situations in your life that you are looking at from a natural, human perspective? What would the above the sun perspective be?

9. Is it wrong for a Christian to desire things that are not spiritual, such as a home, car, money?

10. Describe the abundant life Christ has made available to those who belong to Him. Has your definition changed since reading the Introduction and first chapter of this book? If so, how?

11. How was Eve deceived? Explain the danger of dissatisfaction to a marriage, in parenting, with a job, to your church? Think of other examples in the Bible, your life, or the life of someone you know, where dissatisfaction brought trouble or even catastrophe.

Prayer

Father, I surrender my dreams and commit my life to You. Fill me and satisfy me. Cause me to delight myself in You, experiencing Your heart as my own. I ask and thank You for the dreams and desires that are Your plan and purpose for my life. I thank You to bring them to pass according to Psalm 37:4-5. In Jesus' name, I pray.

Confession

I no longer dream dreams with no purpose. I seek God as my Source for all I am and all I need. His desires are becoming my own.

Chapter 2 ───────────────────────────

Restraining Wandering Hearts
─────────────────────────────────────

He feeds on ashes, a deluded heart misleads him;
he cannot save himself, or say,
"Is not this thing in my right hand a lie?
Isaiah 44:20

God has put in our fallen nature a desire to be fulfilled and to feel complete in order that we would pursue the only One who can fulfill and complete us – Him. Had God not put this longing in our souls, we would have settled for salvation alone without pursuing the intimacy He desires for us now. Therefore, every male and female strives to find contentment in life but many times they wander off the course that leads to it. Because nature abhors a vacuum, when we fail to pursue intimacy with God beyond the salvation experience, we are left vulnerable to the temptation to try to fill the void with things, work, people, our children, and our spouses. We begin to wander further from the place where we would find the thing we really need – the presence of God.

Let me stop and make a point to the married people. If you expect your spouse to fill this emptiness within you, you are expecting them to do the impossible. Your spouse cannot do what only God can do. The sooner we realize this, the better off our marriages will be. The world is tainted by sin and so is every person we know. Therefore, to expect to find satisfaction from anything or anyone other than God is insane. Yet, we sometimes allow our hearts to wander away from the One who created us, focusing our affections elsewhere. God describes our problem in Jeremiah 2:13. He says: *For*

My people have committed two evils: They have forsaken Me, The fountain of living waters, to hew for themselves cisterns, broken cisterns that can hold no water. Those idols may hold a little water. They may satisfy momentarily. But, it is not long before they run dry. Most of us have had the momentary satisfaction of actually receiving that which we yearned so desperately for, only to discover that after a few months of having it, the blessing wore off. We asked, why did I think I could not live without that? Our souls were empty again, in search for something greater, and perhaps even more costly, in an attempt to satisfy the restlessness dwelling deep within.

I remember being eighteen years old and thinking if I could just leave home and get married, that would solve all my problems. I thought it would be the end-all of everything. But once the honeymoon was over, real life problems and challenges began to squeeze into the scene. Not having God in my life at the time, I found myself focused on challenging issues and walking through life disappointed, in search of that perfect thing that would make my life just right. I had not yet found Christ at this time of my life; and I was not drifting in a direction that led to Him. Instead, I was wandering further away from God and I was miserable. To remind myself to guard my time with God, I now choose to remember the emptiness I found back then, no matter what way I turned. I have experienced the reality that nothing in this world can satisfy our craving heart except God.

Isaiah 55:2 (NCV) says it well: *Why spend your money on something that is not real food? Why work for something that doesn't really satisfy you? Listen closely to me, and you will eat what is good; you will enjoy the rich food that satisfies.*

This declaration is telling us that it doesn't make sense to spend our time, money and effort trying to discover satisfaction from anything of this world. Only God has the nourishment that truly satisfies; whereas, idols are empty and void of any real nourishment. We are told in Matthew 4:4 (AMP): *Man shall not live and be upheld and sustained by bread alone, but by every word that comes forth from the mouth of God.* Our physical bodies are satisfied when properly nourished. The same is true of our spirit where our longing lies. It can only be satisfied with that which is proper nourishment for it—the Word imparted by the Holy Spirit Himself. John 1:1 informs us that God and the Word of God are one and the same.

Many people think of idolatry as praying to statues. That indeed is a form of idolatry and one that was very common in our biblical examples. The worship of anything God has created – the sun, moon and stars as well as trees, animals and serpents is the worship of false gods. Today, we have new forms of false Gods with our heart's greed and self-focus being at the top of the list. In reality, idolatry is worship or reverence given to *any* created object or person. It is anything taking the place of God in our thought life, time or pursuit.

> Colossians 3:5 speaks of idolatry: *Therefore consider the members of your earthly body as dead to immorality, impurity, passion, evil desire, and greed, which amounts to idolatry.*

Our communion with God goes beyond just reading and memorizing Scripture. Without communing with God in the Spirit, we do not receive the fullness of the truth of the Word. We need more than head knowledge of Scripture, we need an understanding of and communion with it. Otherwise, we continue to hunger. When we spend time with God in silent contemplative prayer and His written word, and we live in obedience to Him, we are destined to experience God's love. We in turn fall in love with Him. Experiencing God's love is key to our satisfaction.

The psalmist asks of God in Psalm 90:14 (NLT): *Satisfy us in the morning with your unfailing love, so we may sing for joy to the end of our lives.* The Psalmist tells us where satisfaction is found – in God's love. He tells us what it does – it causes us to sing for joy, in not only our good days, but also in our bad. Satisfaction begins and ends with receiving God's unfailing love as a reality in our life. David knew God's loving mercy was where his hope existed for future blessings and joy that would eventually conquer his days of grief. The same is true for us. God offers us an everlasting love that is incomparable to anything the world can offer. As we are immersed in His love, our sorrows dissipate, and our souls become truly satisfied.

Sadly, I have met many people who have not been able to experience the love of God simply because of false teachings or a misunderstanding regarding God's love and His amazing grace. So I ask you today, "Do you know His love? Have you received it as a reality into your innermost being? Do you understand and receive the truth that when Christ died on the cross for you, He knew every sin you would ever commit and He chose to die for you anyway?" There is nothing you have done or can do to separate you from His love. The blood of Christ paid for every sin you have or ever will commit. Therefore, when you fail and experience conviction from the Holy Spirit, repent and receive God's forgiveness and cleansing. Then move on (1 John 1:9). Leave the past behind. This is the reality of God's love, unfathomable grace and mercy. You can choose to acknowledge God and receive His love or choose to ignore God and live a life where the reality of God's love and forgiveness is never experienced. The second choice is a direct pathway to dissatisfaction.

This is really important to understand. In essence, "the path to dissatisfaction is a path we ourselves *choose* as we fail to spend time with God." It is the result of ignoring Him and refusing to accept His grace towards us. The consequence of this choice is a life of longing and deception. We find ourselves in idolatry and although we do experience a measure of contentment – a kind of emotional uplifting – we soon discover that anything which lifts us will eventually disappoint us with the event of change; therefore, this results in a varying degree of satisfaction. If we continue in this lifestyle, eventually we can find ourselves on a downward spiral traveling further away from God where our hearts begin to harden towards the things of God. We can find ourselves open to more and more deception. Isaiah 44:20 says: *He feeds on ashes, a deluded heart misleads him; he cannot save himself, or say, "Is not this thing in my right hand a lie?"*

This verse is saying that those who have something, or someone, on the throne of their heart, a place meant only for God, will not find what they are really seeking. They will be like the person who seeks food only to find dust or ashes. How disappointing! How frustrating! The lie in the right hand is referring to their deceptive idol, whether it be a skill, their work, a material item or a host of other things. The point is, it is unable to satisfy or save them from their misery. *A deluded heart misleads him* – the heart is the source of the difficulty. It is first deceived, then the understanding is darkened and the person finds themselves in idolatry.

Romans 6:16 is also emphasizing to us the danger of idols. As we taste the sweetness of even temporary satisfaction through a substitute, even though it will soon turn sour, the desire for that substitute only increases and we begin to chase after that particular substitute even more. There is no end—there is no fulfillment to the desire. The desire continues to increase more and more and our soul remains restless and enslaved. Our quality of life continues to slip away. This explains what happens to the addict whether he craves sex, pornography, alcohol, drugs, food, or even an excessive need for attention at any cost. The artificial sweetness in our God-substitutes soon holds us in bondage as we begin to need even more of that substitute for the same sense of fulfillment we once received from less. This is the spiraling effect of idolatry. When you live for the world instead of God's purposes, your perspective on life is skewed and results in disappointment and sin (Isaiah 5:13, Romans 6:16).

This statement focuses on the wanting, craving condition of man's heart; and, instead of calling the object of the heart the idol, calls the heart itself idolatrous. In other words, Paul is pointing out our tendency to become our own idol, putting our self above God and others. We may turn to greed and immorality simply because of our own selfish desires. Many times we become the objects of our own false worship. Our fear of death and rejection from men is a result of our self-focus and worship of self, as are all our insecurities. The truth is, without freedom from fear of men, insecurity, death and rejection, there can be no satisfaction.

You may be asking, how do we keep ourselves from falling into idolatry? First Corinthians 10:13-15 says: *No temptation has overtaken you except what is common to mankind. And God is faithful; he will not let you be tempted beyond what you can bear. But when you are tempted, he will also provide a way out so that you can endure it. Therefore, my dear friends, flee from idolatry. I speak to sensible people; judge for yourselves what I say.* The answer is, you flee it. You ask, "But how do we flee from idolatry?"

James 4:8 gives us the answer. We are to *draw near to God*. As we do, He will draw near to us and supply the grace we need to flee temptation.

God has made everything beautiful in its time. As we pursue Him, He will bring into our lives other things for our enjoyment according to His wisdom and purpose. Mark 10:29 again encourages us to set our hearts on following Christ: *"Truly I tell you,"* Jesus replied, *"no one who has left home or brothers or sisters or mother or father or children or fields for me and the gospel will fail to receive a hundred times as much in this present age: homes, brothers, sisters, mothers, children and fields—along with persecutions—and in the age to come eternal life."* When we seek His kingdom and ways, He takes care of our emptiness and other needs far beyond what we ever could. Therefore, we are to guard our hearts from wandering and allow God to give us all that we need physically, spiritually, emotionally – the friends, the marriage, the job, the awards and promotions, the golf game, the wardrobe, the finances. This is where peace for the restless soul is found—In Christ, trusting God with our lives, surrendering Lordship to Christ. He has made us for Himself and it is He and only He who truly satisfies. Only He is able.

We are told we are to love the Lord God with all of our heart, mind, soul and strength (Matthew 22:37). When we spend time with Him, our love grows. We are taking steps toward experiencing a satisfied life, blessed with the abundance God has for us. It is God who provides for us in every aspect of our lives. He is our source. Our understanding of this comes as we grow in our knowledge of God, who He is – in love, character and power.

As we determine to restrain our wandering hearts and focus our eyes on the eternal rather than the temporal, our perspective aligns with God's perspective regarding materialism and other worldly temptations. Our heart's attachment to the world lessens, and our harmony with God increases. We are satisfied.

Moments at the Fountain

Reflection & Application

Things to Remember

- The restless soul learns contentment as the heart stays focused on Christ and things of the spirit.

- As we pursue God and His love as first priority in our lives, His love satisfies our restless souls.

- The sweet taste in our God-substitutes soon turns sour as our need for that substitute increases for the same sense of fulfillment we once received from less.

- Ignoring God results in losing an awareness of His love which results in dissatisfaction. Therefore, ignoring God is *choosing* to be dissatisfied.

- Without freedom from fear of men, insecurity, death and rejection, there can be no satisfaction.

- People and things that we dream about can bring real happiness to our souls *only* when God has given them to us. He is the only *true source* for all that we need.

Jeremiah 2:13

> *"My people have committed two sins: They have forsaken me, the spring of living water, and have dug their own cisterns, broken cisterns that cannot hold water."*

Isaiah 44:19-20

> *" ...Shall I bow down to a block of wood?"*
> *Such a person feeds on ashes; a deluded heart misleads him;*
> *he cannot save himself, or say,*
> *"Is not this thing in my right hand a lie?"*

Matthew 6:33 (NASB)

> *Seek first the kingdom of God and His righteousness and all these things will be given to you.*

Psalm 90:14 (NLT)

> *Satisfy us in the morning with your unfailing love, so we may sing for joy to the end of our lives.*

Reflect & Grow

1. Take a moment and think honestly about yourself. What is it that you find yourself desiring more of? As it increases in your life, have you noticed you only want more? It could be money, success, more things. What does the Scripture call this condition?

2. Read Exodus 20:2-5. How does God describe idolatry in this passage?

3. What is idolatry? What happens to someone when they fall into idolatry? What can they do to find freedom again?

4. Look at Isaiah 55:2. What does it say about riches and satisfaction?

5. What does the author attribute the dissatisfaction found in the body of Christ to? Give some examples you have witnessed that support this statement.

6. According to Psalm 16:11, where do we find fullness of joy?

7. Genuine satisfaction is available to those who _____ and
   _____ .

8. What two things are necessary in order to experience the abundant
   life? See 1 Timothy 6:6.

9. Describe the cycle of deception? Read Isaiah 5:12-13 and Romans
   6:16.

10. According to Psalm 90:14 how is it we are satisfied? What importance
    do you think there might be to the word "morning" used in this Scrip-
    ture instead of "night"?

Prayer

*Father, thank You for your love and patience towards me. Thank
You for the promises and the hope You have given me in Christ
Jesus. Help me Lord to keep You first priority in my life and to
focus my thoughts on You and the reality of Your presence in my
life. Help me to grow in an experiential knowledge of You and the
power of God available to me in Christ Jesus that I may walk in
Your ways and be satisfied. In Jesus' name, I pray.*

Confession

*I no longer live with a wandering heart. I live my life with
purpose, staying focused on Christ.*

Chapter 3 ————————————————————————

Resisting Worrisome Ways

Do not be anxious about anything, but in
everything, by prayer and petition, with
thanksgiving, present your requests to God.
Philippians 4:6

Anyone struggle with anxiety? Do you ever worry about things you have no control over? Well, I do. Not as much as I use to, but in certain situations, I still at times find myself anxious.

Since we are living in a fallen world, we are faced with challenges that, if we are not careful, can overtake us with anxiety and distract us away from the source of what we need. False rumors or gossip that threatens to damage our reputations, illness, surgeries, life-threatening disease in our life or the life of a loved one, children's challenging attitudes, strained marriages, stressed work environments, mounting bills, loss of income, and many other challenges can threaten our satisfaction as we take them on as burdens, to carry ourselves, instead of turning them over to God. The truth is, we were not created in such a way to carry these burdens; on the other hand, they are no problem for Christ. He implores us in Matthew 11:28-30: *Come to me, all you who are weary and burdened, and I will give you rest. Take my yoke upon you and learn from me, for I am gentle and humble in heart, and you will find rest for your souls. For my yoke is easy and my burden is light.*

It is impossible to live satisfied if we are anxious. Worrying steals our sense of fulfillment and satisfaction. It can enslave us and steal our health as well. You may have heard the saying, "You don't get ulcers from what you eat... You get ulcers from what is eating you."[7] We are not the only ones who have had to conquer this sin. The great theologian, John Calvin himself, was prone to anxiety. He spoke about those who are extremely anxious, saying, "They wear themselves out and become their own executioners."[8]

As we again look at the Apostle Paul's life, we see that he faced trials that for most of us, in comparison, make our worst days seem good. He suffered persecution in all forms and levels from false allegations to beatings. For example, while in prison and faced with the possibility of execution, people were spreading dangerous rumors about Paul. Some even claimed to be Christians, but they were damaging Paul's reputation as a man of God. Some of their talk caused Paul to suffer even more persecution. Although you yourself may not have experienced beatings for your faith, perhaps you have experienced false charges at some level. It is not uncommon for Christians who are truly dedicated to Christ to find themselves with this type of mistreatment; and, anxiety, many times, comes along with it.

I think we can agree that Paul definitely had reason, humanly speaking, to be anxious. Yet, Paul was not worried. Paul's attitude was: *For me to live is Christ and to die is gain* (Philippians 1:21). He not only died to his concern of his reputation, trusting God's hand on His life, he was also prepared to die physically in order to be with Christ. Yet, if it was Christ's will he live on earth a while longer, he was willing to for the furtherance of the gospel and to help the Philippians in their spiritual journey.

What was it about Paul that allowed him to maintain his satisfaction and hold this noble attitude in the midst of all his afflictions? The following habits are clearly seen in Paul throughout his New Testament letters, and help to answer this question —

First: Paul was totally surrendered to God's purpose for his life.

He understood the eternal plan and purpose of God was much greater than any temporal purpose he could dream up. He knew God's purpose was beyond what his human mind was able to comprehend. God speaks to us through Isaiah 55:9: *As the heavens are higher than the earth, so are my ways higher than your ways and my thoughts than your thoughts.* Once you accept this truth, you can surrender and quit trying to figure out God's reasoning, and rest in Him and His plan for your life.

Second: Paul trusted God's love and control over his life.

Paul realized that no man or circumstance could take his reputation or his life unless God allowed it. He accepted that God is sovereign, all-powerful, all-knowing, always present, and that God had the power and authority to work out His plan through the lives of those on earth, to include his own. In other words, Paul was satisfied in God's love, and trusting of His ability and faithfulness in managing the affairs of his life. God's sovereign involvement gave purpose to every situation Paul found himself in. His attitude reminds me of the account in John 19:10-11 when Christ stood in front of Pilate. Pilate said: *Don't you realize I have power either to free you or to crucify you?* Christ responded: *You would have no power over me if it were not given to you from above...*

Like Jesus, Paul understood that no man, demon, or circumstance had power over him. The same is true for all Christians. If things are headed in a direction that God cannot use to fulfill His purpose, then He will change the direction in which they are headed. Nothing is going to happen unless it can be used in the accomplishment of God's eternal plan. It is God's *yes* or *no* that determines destiny. He is in control. What peace indwells my soul as I meditate on these truths.

Third: Paul focused on the reality of eternity and his rewards in Christ.

Once Paul's decision was made to live surrendered to God's purpose and plan, and to trust His sovereign authority and control, he was able to direct his focus from temporary circumstances to the reality of eternal rewards. He realized his circumstances and earthly rewards held no comparison to those that are eternal. This resulted in supernatural peace for Paul, even in the midst of chaos. We, too, can have God's peace in our lives, knowing that regardless of the concerns that surround us, they are nothing compared to the glory that awaits us. We are able to be content in any situation as we view it from the perspective of eternity.

Matthew 6:25-40 informs us that as the righteousness of God in Christ, we are the partakers of divine riches. One of those divine riches is the

strength of Christ for every situation (Philippians 4:13). If you know you have God's power on your side and you know God will meet *all* your needs, then why would you worry? Anxiousness is a small trickle of fear that twists and turns through the mind until it forms a furrow into which all other thoughts are drained. "Worry is a form of atheism, for it betrays a lack of faith and trust in God" (attributed to Bishop Fulton J. Sheen).[9] On the other hand, the righteous who trust in God are described in Psalm 1:3 as being:
...like a tree planted by the rivers of water, that brings forth its fruit in its season, whose leaf also shall not wither; and whatever he does shall prosper.
As we view our circumstances through the lens of eternity, our trust increases and we are strengthened for any and every situation that presents itself in our life.

Fourth: Paul prayed and maintained a grateful heart.

Exhorting the Philippians, Paul gives them simple steps to eliminate worry. Philippians 4:6-7: *Be anxious for nothing, but in everything by **prayer** and **supplication**, with **thanksgiving**, let your requests be made known to God; and the peace of God, which surpasses all understanding, will guard your hearts and minds through Christ Jesus* (emphasis mine). Without prayer, you will worry. When we pray, we are releasing our fears and worries to God. We are saying to Him, "I put my trust in You." As we do this, His peace floods our souls, as He guides us as to what we should do, if anything.

Philippians 4:6 also mentions supplication. Supplication is praying with intense fervor. It is an earnest appeal, with recognition of one's need for God's intervention. It is crying out with humility, beseeching God for His help. We then are instructed to add to our prayer and supplication a thankful heart as we thank God for the goodness, mercy and faithfulness He has already shown towards us. As we give thanks to the Lord for what He has done for us already – our salvation in Christ and all He has brought us through in the past – our thoughts are refocused on God, His power and faithfulness. Thank Him for all those times that seemed impossible; yet, He brought you through. Thank Him as your tower of refuge and strength and for His wisdom, power and sovereign love. As we refocus on God – His love, character and ability – instead of our circumstances and extremely limited power, our worries begin to diminish. We are at peace knowing He is sure to intervene and do what is best for us. We have the expectation to see Him answer our current need according to His divine wisdom simply because of His love and mercy towards us who are His.

There is no situation in which we need to be anxious or fearful. There is no situation we cannot take to the throne room of grace, whether it is a situation existing because of our own sin, failure, or poor choice; or, a situation that exists due to something outside of ourselves. We are told to bring it *all* to God with prayer, supplication and thanksgiving. As we do this, we exchange our burdens for God's supernatural yoke of peace. We discover that His yoke is light, indeed.

Fifth: Paul looked at his present circumstances in light of the promises of God for his future.

To apply God's promises to life's situations requires intentional, conscious effort and either memorization of Scripture or searching the Scriptures to find the word God has for your current situation, or both. It also requires self-discipline to focus your attention on God versus your circumstances. When we are tempted to think contrary to what God has promised, we should take our thoughts captive to the obedience of Christ (2 Corinthians 10:5), and insist on thinking thoughts that are true, noble, right, pure, lovely, admirable, excellent and praiseworthy (Philippians 4:8). When you learn to take your thoughts captive and intentionally meditate on God's promises, you will find peace and satisfaction. When you are going through a difficult season, you may want to carry some scripture cards with you or place them in handy places in your home to remind you of God's faithfulness to bring you through.

Another way to protect your mind from becoming entrapped with worry is to *speak* the promises of God. The Bible informs us that the words of life and death are in the tongue (Proverbs 18:21). Jesus says in John 6:63: *It is the Spirit who gives life; the flesh profits nothing; the words that I have spoken to you are spirit and are life.* When you speak thoughts that enter your mind that are contrary to the Word of God, those thoughts become more deeply rooted in your mind and affect your feelings, actions and life.

Whereas, speaking the Word of God results in faith taking root in your mind, will and emotions. The spoken Word of God imparts life and peace, and you become satisfied.

When we have desires that appear not to be progressing, we must remember that our goals will be met by the grace of God; and, only if they are in the perfect plan of God; and, we must remember that they will happen in God's perfect timing, not necessarily in the time frame we have planned. Our days are held in His hands and only He knows what tomorrow holds; so, we should keep our eyes on doing what we can do today. I see people worry about things that might happen in the future to upset their lives and dreams. When the future arrives, all is well. What a waste of energy and thought life! It is so much wiser to live by Matthew 6:34: *Therefore do not worry about tomorrow, for tomorrow will worry about itself. Each day has enough trouble of its own.* We must guard our minds against worries about the days ahead if we want to be content today. Besides, God promises to take care of us in a greater way than He clothes the grass of the field or feeds the birds of the air. Matthew 7:25-30:

> *Therefore I tell you, do not worry about your life, what you will eat or drink; or about your body, what you will wear. Is not life more than food, and the body more than clothes? Look at the birds of the air; they do not sow or reap or store away in barns, and yet your heavenly Father feeds them. Are you not much more valuable than they? Can any one of you by worrying add a single hour to your life? "And why do you worry about clothes? See how the flowers of the field grow. They do not labor or spin. Yet I tell you that not even Solomon in all his splendor was dressed like one of these. If that is how God clothes the grass of the field, which is here today and tomorrow is thrown into the fire, will he not much more clothe you—you of little faith?*

Matthew Henry shares in his commentary on chapter six of Matthew: "Happy are those who take the Lord for their God, and make full proof of it by trusting themselves wholly to his wise disposal."[10] Why do we worry about things that haven't happened yet? God has given us the promise to be with us. He has provided great riches at our disposal, including his strength and the spiritual armor needed for any battle that may lie ahead for us. We must resign ourselves to the fact that our journey on earth will involve spiritual warfare and suffering at times, and determine to trust God while using the weapons He has put at our disposal. Ephesians 6:10-18 says: *Be strong in the Lord and the strength of His might.* How?... By putting on the whole armor of God. Again, Matthew Henry comments: "Resist him, and he will flee. If we give way, he will get ground. We give way when we distrust our cause, or our Leader, or our armor."[11] Henry goes on to say: "we must commit to God by prayer and patient perseverance in well-doing. He will overrule all to the final advantage of the believer."[12]

Another way to minimize worrisome thoughts is to determine to make the best of every day per Solomon's wisdom to us (Ecclesiastes 11). He encourages us not to take a single day for granted; but instead, to take advantage of the good days when they are good – knowing there will be hard days to come; yet, they will be temporary. Ecclesiastes 11:8 (MSG) describes our troubling days saying: *most of what comes your way is smoke.* We can guard our minds by remembering that every day – the good and bad – is a gift from God providing us with the opportunity to make good of it, while discovering God's grace and purpose in it.

We may not realize it, but worry is a sin against God. It is essentially unbelief, because the Bible says God did not give us a spirit of fear. Second Timothy 1:7 (AMP) explains: *For God did not give us a spirit of timidity (of cowardice, of craven and cringing and fawning fear), but (He has given us a spirit) of power and of love and of calm and well-balanced mind and discipline and self-control.* When we worry, we are not in possession of a calm, balanced mind. Interestingly, James 1:6-8 refers to the person who teeters back and forth between doubt and faith, as double minded. It declares that because of their unstable ways, they should not expect to receive anything from God.

Many people mistakenly think that fear is the opposite of faith, when it is sight that is the opposite of faith. Love is the opposite of fear as we clearly see from 2 Timothy 1:7. Therefore, although it is a good thing to memorize Scripture, we need to understand that memorization in itself is not what ignites our faith. Let me explain. Our faith is expanded when we hear a "rhema" word from God – when God speaks to us personally, imparting direction or comfort to us for a particular situation (Romans 10:17). When this happens, the words that you may have read many times over again, become more than mere head knowledge. You just heard from God and you know it, so your faith naturally expands. However, we can lack the motivation or energy to move on the Word of God if we are not filled with the love of God, returning it back toward God and toward others. Although the Word of God is the sword of the Spirit, and it is what we fight our battles with, it is love that fortifies our faith and propels us into action.

Although faith comes as a result of hearing the Word of God, love is the key ingredient that makes everything work. You are most likely familiar with the "love" chapter (1 Corinthians, chapter thirteen) in the Bible. It clearly states we are nothing without love, no matter how much faith we have. That is because without love, our faith lies dormant, allowing fear and complacency to trickle in. Scripture tells us that *perfect love casts out fear* (1 John 4:18). Again, where love exists, fear does not.

As we grow in our experiential knowledge of God's love and our love towards God and others, that love puts feet to our faith. Galatians 5:6 (AMP) puts it this way: *For (if we are) in Christ Jesus, neither circumcision nor uncircumcision counts for anything, but only faith activated and energized and expressed and working through love…* I believe there are many Christians who are working on their faith walk when they need to work on their love walk. Perhaps when we get our love walk right, our faith will be there.

When I lack faith, I ask myself, how am I doing in my love walk? Am I confident in the love God has for me? Is my love for God and others apparent? Hebrews 11:6 says: *And without faith it is impossible to please God, because anyone who comes to him must believe that he exists and that he rewards those who earnestly seek him.* Worry and fear flee as our faith is energized by love. God is pleased and we are satisfied.

Here's an example of how love energizes our faith: Someone may hear from God through one of the various ways God communicates to us – through Scripture or the person of the Holy Spirit. He may ask them to do something that requires them to put their popularity with others at risk in order to support or save someone who is being treated unfairly. If that person lacks in love, they may not act on God's Word to them. Instead of allowing the Spirit of God to lead them, they are led by the spirit of fear. God's love perfected in us is the force behind our faith, setting it in motion, activating and energizing it (Galatians 5:6). Where there is love, there is faith in action.

John 3:16 expresses the ultimate *love* God has for us. He sent His only begotten Son, Jesus Christ, to save us from our sin and eternal damnation. God's love has been proven and we can put our trust in Him. Nahum 1:7 (NKJV) declares God's care in the midst of difficult circumstances: *The LORD is good, a stronghold in the day of trouble, and He knows those who trust in Him.* Also, Lamentations 3:22-23: *Through the LORD's mercies we are not consumed, because His compassions fail not. They are new every morning; great is Your faithfulness.* Jeremiah 29:11 tells us of God's good plans for us. And, Philippians 4:19 declares that God will supply our every need according to His riches in glory in Christ Jesus. Why worry? God cares for us! When we trust Him, we will never be disappointed.

We can make the most of our days, rejoicing in both trials and joyful times without knowing God's plan in them, as long as we understand that He does have a purpose for what He allows or brings into our lives. We learn from God's Word to us, for instance, that our trials teach us, equip us, and mold us into the person God has destined us to be. Romans 8:28-29 says: *And we know that in all things God works for the good of those who love him, who have been called according to his purpose. For those God foreknew he also predestined to be conformed to the likeness of his Son, that he might be the firstborn among many brothers.*

We also know that when we are in a difficult season of life, it will come to an end. We have hope through Scriptures such as Psalm 30:5 that joy will soon invade us: *For His anger is but for a moment, His favor is for a lifetime; Weeping may last for the night, but a shout of joy comes in the morning...* Nothing lasts forever on this earth! Joy does come – maybe not twenty-four hours later – but the trial will one day end, if not this side of heaven, on the other. This truth – that our suffering will not last forever – is especially important to remember during times of extreme suffering. Revelation 14:13 (NKJV): *Blessed are those who die in the LORD from now on. Yes, says the*

Spirit, they are blessed indeed, for they will rest from all their toils and trials; for their good deeds follow them!

It is important to understand that God doesn't promise us that we will be free of trials and tribulations. In fact, He promises just the opposite. He promises we will have them. Jesus says in John 16:33: ... *I have told you these things, so that in me you may have peace. In this world you will have trouble. But take heart! I have overcome the world.* This verse lets us know we can expect those bad days, as Solomon said. But it also lets us know that we are ensured victory because Christ's victory is ours. Therefore, while in the midst of a trial, we can shout with thanksgiving because we hold victory in our sight. Second Corinthians 2:14 encourages us: *But thanks be to God, who always leads us in triumph in Christ, and manifests through us the sweet aroma of the knowledge of Him in every place.* We can do anything required of us as we depend on Christ's strength and power instead of our own (Philippians 4:13).

We can also reduce the opportunity for anxiety in our lives by making changes that may be needed. For instance, if I am fretting over the bills, I might want to implement a change in our family budget and lifestyle. Perhaps you are concerned about your health. I recently found myself worrying about the rise in my blood pressure. I went to the doctor to get his help in putting together a low-calorie diet. I lost ten pounds and my blood pressure immediately returned to normal. Taking steps to improve the particular area of life that is giving you concern can help bridge the gap between worry and faith.

To close this chapter, I want to make my last point by sharing a short story. It goes like this:

"I have a mountain of credit card debt," one man told another.

"I've lost my job, my car is being repossessed, and our house is in foreclosure, but I'm not worried.

"Not worried about it!" exclaimed his friend.

"No. I've hired a professional worrier. He does all my worrying for me, and that way I don't have to think about it."

"That's fantastic. How much does your professional worrier charge for his services?"

"Fifty thousand dollars a year," replied the first man.

"Fifty thousand dollars a year! Where are you going to get that kind of money?"

"I don't know," came the reply. "That's his worry!"

In a sense, the Lord's servants do have a professional worrier to do all our worrying for us. As 1 Peter 5:7 (Phillips) says: *You can throw the whole weight of your anxieties upon him, for you are his personal concern.*[13]

So what are the concerns you have today? Whether it is paying the bills, raising your children, making a decision about a company move and promotion, your health or the health of a loved one, seek the kingdom of God and His righteousness (Luke 12:31), make your requests known to God with thanksgiving, and He will keep your heart at rest.

Moments at the Fountain

Reflection & Application

Things to Remember

- The restless are satisfied when faith rises in God's sovereign love, ability, and willingness to care for them no matter what the circumstance.

- Prayer with supplication and thanksgiving results in peace. A peaceful, thankful heart results in satisfaction.

- God's love perfected in us is the force behind our faith, setting it in motion, activating, and energizing it.

- Without living by faith, it is impossible to be satisfied.

- Satisfaction is imminent as we guard our minds by: (1) Praying with thanksgiving (2) Focusing on Christ, eternity & our riches in Christ (3) Taking thoughts captive to God's perspective based on His promises (4) Speaking words of life.

- When I am thanking God, my thoughts are focused on God and His character instead of my troubles or shortcomings.

- Speaking the Word of God causes faith to take root in our hearts.

- Fear and love are opposites. Where fear is, love lacks. Faith and sight are opposites. Where faith is needed, there is no sight. Faith is realized in the midst of our blindness.

John 19:11

You would have no power over me if it were not given to you from above...

Philippians 4:19

...my God will meet all (my) needs according to his glorious riches in Christ Jesus.

1 John 4:18 (NLT)

Such love has no fear, because perfect love expels all fear. If we are afraid, it is for fear of punishment, and this shows that we have not fully experienced his perfect love.

Philippians 4:6-7

Be anxious for nothing, but in everything by prayer and supplication, with thanksgiving, let your requests be made known to God; and the peace of God, which surpasses all understanding, will guard your hearts and minds through Christ Jesus.

Galatians 5:6 (AMP)

For [if we are] in Christ Jesus, neither circumcision nor uncircumcision counts for anything, but only faith activated and energized and expressed and working through love...

Romans 8:28 (NLT)

And we know that God causes everything to work together for the good of those who love God and are called according to his purpose for them.

Matthew 11:29 (NIV)

Take my yoke upon you and learn from me, for I am gentle and humble in heart, and you will find rest for your souls.

Reflect & Grow

1. You may want to start writing down your thoughts and reviewing them to see what kind of pattern is in your thinking. What thoughts have you been dwelling on regularly? Are they thoughts that lead to worry or to faith in God? How can you find satisfaction when applying Luke 19:10 to those worrisome thoughts?

2. What do you do when worry arises? What can you do to change the habits you have formed in dealing with concerns and trials that have not led to satisfaction?

3. What areas of your life have you allowed to get out of control by focusing on the situations of worry more than Christ's provision? What can you do to turn that around?

4. What does Philippians 4:7 say happens when we make our requests known to God? What three elements are to be present in this request?

5. What are five things you can do to guard your mind from worry and anxious thinking?

6. How does an understanding of the sovereignty of God in your life affect you? Discuss your feelings and help one another to find the peace available to experience when this truth is recognized.

7. What areas of life have you failed to trust God? Confess your lack of trust in God as sin, ask for forgiveness and ask Him to help you to develop new behavior patterns to implement change in your lifestyle. Ask Him to show you how to trust Him.

8. Why is worry a sin against God? Read Hebrews 11:6.

9. Do you believe God is in control of your bad times as well as good – sovereign over all that happens in the world from devastations to blessings? Share some biblical examples.

10. What is the opposite of faith? When can we see our faith in action? See pages 45 and 46.

11. What are you fearful of? What does 2 Timothy 1:7 say about fear?

12. What is the opposite of fear? What steps can you take to increase your faith and eliminate fear?

13. How does Habakkuk 3:17-19 relieve your worries and bring you comfort?

Prayer

Father, thank You for filling me with Your love that I may return it to You and to others. I hold tightly to Your promises and I release my worries and burdens to You, trusting and resting in You. Thank You for every good and perfect gift in my life and meeting the needs that only You can meet. Thank You for speaking to me personally and giving me faith to endure the difficult seasons of life. I rejoice knowing that You care for me, equip me and walk with me through every trial. In Jesus' name, I pray.

Confession

I no longer worry. I trust in the Lord's sovereign love and power; therefore, I'm able to rest from all my concerns.

Chapter 4 ────────────────────

Opposing the World's View

────────────────────────────────

*They have harps and lyres at their banquets, tambourines
and flutes and wine, but they have no regard for the deeds
of the LORD, no respect for the work of his hands.*

Isaiah 5:12

The definition for satisfaction according to *The American Heritage College Dictionary* is a) The fulfillment or gratification of a desire, need, or appetite, and b) Pleasure or contentment derived from such gratification.[14]

Contentment from the world's view involves the possessing, indulging, hoarding, or obtaining of something outside of one's self. The world's view of contentment teaches that we receive contentment from people: "If I could just hang out with so and so…" But people never live up to our expectations. The world teaches contentment comes from positions and awards: "If I could just get the right job…" But what happens when we lose the job due to a company shut down or lay-off? The world stresses the importance of things to our satisfaction: "When I get my new car… or new house…then, I will be content." But nothing stays new for long. And, trophies – they grow rusty.

The Christian who lives by the world's view of satisfaction is living with highs and lows because their level of satisfaction is affected by external sources such as people, position and material items – all subject to change. The popular American expression which speaks of 'keeping up with the Joneses,' – that is, having as many material possessions as your neighbors, is often practiced in the church as well as in the world. It is unfortunate to see Christians trying to upstage one another in this way. In this race to see who can outdo whom, contentment is, indeed, lost.

Twenty-first century marketing techniques have not helped the situation; although, this is not the root of our problem. After all, dissatisfaction was around a long time before modern day promotional methods. However, the world does feed our self-centered desires with a constant bombardment of advertising from billboards, the Internet, and television commercials. All these advertisements promise happiness but focus our attention on ourselves and our wants to such a level that it is *not having* what is advertised that leaves us unhappy, unfulfilled and depressed. First Timothy 6:10 says: *For the love of money is a root of all kinds of evil. Some people, eager for money, have wandered from the faith and pierced themselves with many griefs.* The pursuit of things at all costs, only results in grief. And a constant inward focus results in the same.

We try to quench our thirst for more of God with substitutes that come in many different forms. I will say it again, if you live by faith in yourself and what you can do, or by faith in someone else and what they can do for you, or by faith in anything and what it can do for you, you will be disappointed. As discussed earlier, when you try to satisfy your emptiness from any source other than God, the experience is counterfeit and will disappoint, deceive, and slowly begin to hold you captive. In this state, although you are saved, the truly abundant life God has for you awaits somewhere in the distance and you are dissatisfied.

Look at Isaiah 5:12-13: *They have harps and lyres at their banquets, tambourines and flutes and wine, but they have no regard for the deeds of the Lord, no respect for the work of his hands. Therefore my people will go into exile for lack of understanding; their men of rank will die of hunger and their masses will be parched with thirst.*

In this scripture, their music and alcohol is a counterfeit experience of satisfaction. They carry on as though they will live forever in their sinful ways, not giving any thought or honor to God for His provision for their lives. However, they are sadly mistaken and they find their satisfaction soon comes to an end. Genuine satisfaction, on the other hand, cannot be changed from external sources. Genuine satisfaction is internal and eternal. And, it has no regrets in eternity.

Like most everything else in the world – the world's view of satisfaction is focused on self, instead of on God and others. It is about *me* getting and doing what *I* want, even though it only results in temporary fulfillment. *Even in laughter the heart may ache, and joy may end in grief* (Proverbs 14:13). In this state of dissatisfaction, one cannot experience true abundance or the fullness of the destiny God has for them. On the other hand, when we turn to God as the Fountain of Living Waters, He satisfies our soul. First Timothy, chapter six, goes on to encourage us to flee our pursuit of God-substitutes. *But you, man of God, flee from all this, and pursue righteousness, godliness, faith, love, endurance and gentleness. Fight the good fight of the faith. Take hold of the eternal life to which you were called when you made your good confession in the presence of many witnesses.* As we flee from our counterfeit sources to pursue the one true source for all that we need and desire, we will declare to God, as did the psalmist: *You open Your hand and satisfy the desire of every living thing (Psalm 145:16).*

Moments at the Fountain

Reflection & Application

Things to Remember

- The restless soul cannot be satisfied by a change in external circumstances but only by the internal presence of the eternal God. He is the Fountain of Living Waters and the only One who can satisfy the longings in our soul.

- To live by faith in what you can do, what someone else can do or in what anything or anyone can do for you will result in disappointment.

- When you try to satisfy your emptiness from any source other than God, the thing you experience will deceive you and begin to hold you captive to an insatiable need.

Isaiah 5:12

They have harps and lyres at their banquets, tambourines and flutes and wine, but they have no regard for the deeds of the LORD, no respect for the work of his hands.

1 Timothy 6:10-12

> *For the love of money is a root of all kinds of evil. Some people, eager for money, have wandered from the faith and pierced themselves with many griefs. But you, man of God, flee from all this, and pursue righteousness, godliness, faith, love, endurance and gentleness. Fight the good fight of the faith. Take hold of the eternal life to which you were called when you made your good confession in the presence of many witnesses.*

Psalm 145:16

> *You open Your hand and satisfy the desire of every living thing.*

Reflect & Grow

1. What is the world's view of satisfaction? Where does the world say you can find it?

2. How does the world feed our self-centered desires?

3. How can you avoid the deceptive trap of needing to keep up with the Joneses?

4. Have you ever put on smiles and laughter but inside there was restlessness, dissatisfaction and a lack of true joy? Is this masked appearance a struggle for transparency or are we deceiving ourselves that everything is fine?

5. Have you forsaken God as the Fountain of Living Waters? List the substitutes you look to in search of satisfaction. This may include anything that brings you a sense of significance, acceptance, power, importance or worthiness outside of your relationship with God. After identifying these things, follow the instructions found in 1 John 1:9.

6. Genuine satisfaction cannot be affected by external sources. Genuine satisfaction is internal and eternal. Consider and discuss these statements.

7. If you live by faith in yourself and what you can do or by faith in someone else and what they can do for you, or by faith in any thing and what it can do for you, you will be disappointed. Think about your life. Do you find yourself in any of these places? What can you do to begin making a change in this area?

8. Share a time when you found yourself disappointed because you had faith in what you, someone or something could do for you, without considering God as the source for your provision.

9. Why is satisfaction from anything other than God temporary?

10. How is it that the pursuit of things can result in grief? Read 1 Timothy 6:10.

Prayer

I thank You, Father, that You are my source for every thing that pertains to this life and godliness. Thank You for teaching me. Thank you for replacing counterfeit contentment with the genuine, as You open Your hand and satisfy my soul. Thank You for leading me into righteousness for Your name's sake. Keep me from the world's deception and temptations as You supply my every need as I seek first Your Kingdom and righteousness. In Jesus' name, I pray.

Confession

I am not deceived by the world's ideas and lusts; but, I am genuinely satisfied by the hand of God as I experience His internal presence within me.

Chapter 5 —

Embracing the Biblical View

I am not saying this because I am in need, for I have
learned to be content whatever the circumstances.

Philippians 4:11

*W*hen scripture speaks of being content, it means being wholly complete and sufficient – physically, emotionally and spiritually – needing absolutely nothing. *The Holman Bible Dictionary* defines contentment as "an internal satisfaction which does not demand changes in external circumstances."[15] Can you imagine this? As we have already seen, it is evident from the book of Philippians that Paul was one who experienced this. He says in Philippians 4:11: *I am not saying this because I am in need, for I have learned to be content whatever the circumstances.*

A lesson to glean from this passage is that Paul is willing to *accept* those things he cannot change. He is willing to accept the life God has given him. If we are to experience *real* satisfaction, we must learn to do the same. You may say, "But, I am in a marriage with an unbeliever who is rude and has the worst personality on the face of this earth. He or she is impossible to live with." Or, "People have falsely persecuted and lied about me. How can I accept that?"

Hebrews 13:5 exhorts us to depend on God's promise not to forsake His people regardless the situation they find themselves. Hebrews 13:15 says: *Through Jesus, therefore, let us continually offer to God a sacrifice of praise—the fruit of lips that confess His name.* As Christians, we can choose to live by faith in ourselves and the circumstances that surround us, or we can live by faith in a sovereign, all-powerful and loving God! It is a no-brainer. Choose God. Trust in His promise not to forsake you.

To focus on our past which cannot be changed, or our circumstances today that are out of our control, has no benefit to our lives or to our relationship with God. God is sovereign in how He brought us into the world and He has ordained that we live by faith and not by sight. Matthew reminds us that God takes care of the sparrows so He will take much more care of us. Our God is a God of redemption and restoration and we can trust Him to redeem and restore. Just as He restored the loss of children, possessions and health to Job in the Book of Job, He can restore our losses as well. You remember the story in Job 42:10: *After Job had prayed for his friends, the Lord made him prosperous again and gave him twice as much as he had before.* As we trust in God and His sovereignty, we are enabled to persevere. *Indeed we count them blessed who endure. You have heard of the perseverance of Job and seen the end intended by the Lord—that the Lord is very compassionate and merciful* (James 5:11).

God will even take our mistakes and make good of them when we love Him and are called according to His purpose (Romans 8:28), just as He did with Rahab the Harlot. One day, when the Israelites sent spies into Jericho to see how they might take the city, she was presented with an opportunity to help them. She had heard about the power of the Israelites' God and how He favored them. She believed they would, indeed, be successful on their mission in Jericho, so she boldly proclaimed her faith in their God and she made a deal to hide the spies in exchange for her and her family's life. As a result of her faith in God, Rahab and her family were saved during a crisis where there seemed to be no way out. She married an Israelite and became an ancestor of the Lord Jesus Christ. Not only do we see God making good out of what appeared to be impossible circumstances, but we see God made good out of Rahab's past reputation as He exalted her from a harlot to an ancestor of Christ. God can redeem life from your past too!

Look at the story of Joseph in Genesis 35-50. Joseph was given a dream which was God showing him His plans for Joseph's future. In the dream he ruled over his brothers. Joseph's brothers were jealous of their father's evident favoritism of Joseph already; so, after hearing of the dream, they hated him all the more. One day they sold him into slavery. Joseph was purchased from the slave traders by an Egyptian official and he prospered as a servant in his house until, one day, the official's wife accused him of trying to rape her. Joseph ended up in a prison for a crime he did not commit. But even while waiting on God in that prison, the favor of God was on him. All that he put his hand to do was blessed.

Several years later, Joseph interpreted a dream for the Pharaoh who then exalted him by putting him in charge of the whole land of Egypt. Joseph had become the second most powerful man in Egypt, next to the Pharaoh. There was a terrible famine in the land that lasted seven years just as Joseph had predicted. Joseph's brothers came to Egypt seeking food for their family. It was unknown to them that they were seeking help from their brother whom they had sold into slavery. Joseph's brothers repented when they discovered the identity of their brother and they bowed down to him. Joseph's family was saved from the famine because of the position of authority God had exalted Joseph to. Joseph proclaims to his brothers, *But as for you, you meant evil against me; but God meant it for good, in order to bring it about as it is this day, to save many people alive* (Genesis 50:20). God is sovereign and He will use what is meant for evil against us for His good purposes. God has given us promises that we are to stand on, trusting Him in His own timing to bring them to pass.

As mentioned earlier, we see the Apostle Paul rejoicing even while in prison. He was content to know that God was in charge. He was content in knowing what God had done for Him and that his eternal destiny was secure. He trusted the character of God and the sovereignty of God. Paul willed himself to be content and carried his will out in his actions. You see, satisfaction begins with our *acceptance* of God's plan for us regardless the circumstance involved; regardless of people or things; regardless...

In contrast with the world's view of satisfaction, to walk out the biblical definition of satisfaction requires full dependence on what is on the inside of us – almighty God's presence in the person of the Holy Spirit. Just as Paul learned the secret of contentment through his experiences of trials and blessings, you can be initiated into this secret as well. As a Christian, you have the same power residing within you as did Paul, and it is this power of

Christ within that gives spiritual satisfaction. Philippians 4:12-13, *I know what it is to be in need, and I know what it is to have plenty. I have learned the secret of being content in any and every situation, whether well fed or hungry, whether living in plenty or in want. I can do everything through him who gives me strength.*

Just as the roots of a healthy tree are unseen as they grow deep below the surface of the ground, it is through these roots that nourishment flows, strengthening the tree to persevere the harsh elements it will be exposed to. It is this hidden part of the Christian life, which only God sees, that is the most important part of all. It is there that all the power needed to adequately meet the demands of life exists. Through our relationship with God, He nourishes us and supplies the strength we need to weather any storm that comes our way.

A satisfied man or woman is one who keeps God first in their life, recognizing He is the source of everything they need in life. They accept who God has made them to be and the life God has given them. They trust God's love and rule over their life. They rely on God's strength in every situation whether they are in need or in plenty, assured of their eternal security in Christ. Of course, all of these six things are seen in very identifiable external actions. They are worthy for us to take note of:

(1) They are obedient to God's Word (Mark 8:34).

(2) They make time for prayer and Bible study (Matthew 11:29).

(3) They mature spiritually and demonstrate peace in difficult times.

(4) They accept who God has made them to be and the life He has given resounds in their testimony.

(5) They speak of how God has used the challenging circumstances of life and worked them for good. John 19:35 says, *And he who has seen has testified, and his testimony is true; and he knows that he is telling the truth, so that you may believe.*

(6) They serve others. After all, it is because God first loved us that we are able to love Him and all who love Christ love all those who

belong to Him. Therefore, they naturally find themselves serving one another.

God satisfies our soul with His love in our pursuit of Him. It is in the awareness of God's love and our desire to glorify God that springs from our relationship with Him, that we are satisfied. Therefore, to ignore God results in a loss of our experience of His love which then leads to dissatisfaction.

A surrendered heart, content in growing in godliness, is destined for the abundant life. According to 1 Timothy 6:6, *"godliness with contentment is great gain"* (abundance). The abundant satisfied life spoken of in John 10:10 is experienced by those who maintain contentment while being molded by the grace of God through the trials of life into a reflection of Christ. This is the person that no external circumstance or person can shake. This person is fully dependent on God as their source for everything they need for this life and the one to come.

What is happening around you is not as important as your attitude concerning it. Line your attitude up with the promises of God. Let your faith be a rudder to steer you into calmer waters. Ask God to help you recognize and experience the power of Christ within that brings genuine satisfaction. Begin to release that power into your life every morning as you rise. Just as Paul received strength for every situation he found himself in, so will you. And, you will be satisfied.

Since, then, you have been raised with Christ, set your hearts on things above, where Christ is seated at the right hand of God. Set your minds on things above, not on earthly things. For you died, and your life is now hidden with Christ in God. When Christ, who is your life, appears, then you also will appear with him in glory (Colossians 3:1-4).

Moments at the Fountain

Reflection & Application

Things to Remember

- Satisfaction is experienced as we relinquish control and learn how to live in Christ's strength for every challenge of life.

- Acceptance of those things you cannot change is necessary for contentment.

- Satisfaction involves accepting God's plan even when it is not our plan.

- Satisfaction is active. It is seen in the outward actions of obedience, acceptance of life, demonstration of peace, testimonies of God's goodness and service to others.

- Maintaining contentment, while being molded by the grace of God into a reflection of Christ (1 Timothy 6:6), results in the abundant life Christ spoke of in John 10:10.

1 Timothy 6:6
Godliness with contentment is great gain. – The abundant life

Philippians 4:11 (NCV)
I am not telling you this because I need anything. I have learned to be satisfied with the things I have and with everything that happens.

Genesis 50:20

You intended to harm me, but God intended it for good to accomplish what is now being done, the saving of many lives.

Hebrews 13:5

Keep your lives free from the love of money and be content with what you have, because God has said, "Never will I leave you; never will I forsake you."

James 5:11

As you know, we count as blessed those who have persevered. You have heard of Job's perseverance and have seen what the Lord finally brought about. The Lord is full of compassion and mercy.

Hebrews 13:14-15

For here we do not have an enduring city, but we are looking for the city that is to come. Through Jesus, therefore, let us continually offer to God a sacrifice of praise—the fruit of lips that openly profess his name.

Reflect & Grow

1. A Christian, in order to be satisfied, must accept who God is in their life. Consider Psalm 68:7-10, Deuteronomy 4:39, Proverbs 21:1, 1 Samuel 2:6-7 and 12:22. What are some of the things you must accept about God?

2. To be satisfied we need to accept the life God has given us. Consider Leviticus 26:40-43, Psalm 139:13-14, Genesis 1:27, John 16:33, Psalm 68:7-10, 1 Timothy 1:15-17 and Proverbs 3:5-6. What are some things you must accept about your life?

3. What does God have to do with trials and tribulations in our lives? See Psalm 75:7, James 1:2-4, and Romans 5:3-5. Can you accept this truth?

4. Think of situations in your life that God has saved you from. Make a list and refer back to it as a reminder during times when your faith is weak.

5. Let's do an attitude check-up. Think about the following areas of your life and describe your attitude concerning it:

God -   spouse-

children-   church-

job-   heritage-

body-   past circumstances-

present life-

6. If dissatisfied, consider if this is an area that you need to accept as something out of your control. If so, accept God's purpose in it. If not, pray about some goals to set and actions to take to begin moving towards those goals while chiseling away at dissatisfaction.

7. Describe a situation in your life (current or past) where someone was influencing your attitude and you became dissatisfied. How did this affect your behavior? How did it affect your witness of Christ? What can we do to keep our satisfaction in situations such as this?

8. How does the grace of God play into our finding satisfaction?

9. What steps can you take to begin to learn how to be content when you find yourself unfairly treated, betrayed, struggling financially, sick or in the midst of any kind of trial or tribulation?

10. God does have a unique purpose for each individual, however, there is also an overall purpose that each of our individual plans flow into. What is God's ultimate goal for all Christians? Consider Romans 8:28-29.

Prayer

Thank You, Father, for enabling me to be satisfied by teaching me to rely on Your strength when I need to persevere. Thank You for giving me Your wisdom when I need to act upon something that I am faced with in life. Thank You for the genuine contentment and abundance that I have found in Christ Jesus and my relationship with You. Help me to guard my time with You that I may continue to grow in my knowledge and intimacy with You. Thank You that I can rest because I am able to trust You, no matter what. In Jesus' name, I pray.

Confession

By the grace of God, I accept the life God has given me, and I live it in Christ's power & strength – it is Christ in me, my hope of glory!

Chapter 6 ——————————————

Rejoicing Always

These things have I spoken unto you that My joy might remain in you, and that your joy might be full.
John 15:11

Before Jesus faced the cruel and undeserved punishment and death of Calvary, He said to His followers, *These things have I spoken unto you, that My joy might remain in you, and that your joy might be full* (John 15:11). It is a perplexing thing that He could speak of joy knowing what lay ahead in His imminent future. Even as He faced a horrible death, He was content. Jesus desired that His followers possess this same kind of rejoicing in their lives – a joy that even during times of grief, remained.

Remember the story of Naomi and Ruth found in Ruth 1:16-22. At a time when Bethlehem was struck with famine, Naomi and her family, who were Israelites, were forced to move. They settled in Moab where people worshipped a false god called Chemosh. Naomi had two sons, one of which married a Moabite woman named Ruth. Naomi's husband and two sons died. After being gone from Bethlehem for several years, Naomi decided to return. She told Ruth to stay behind but Ruth insisted on honoring Naomi, staying by her mother-in-law's side even though Naomi had not been the most pleasant woman to be with since the death of her husband and sons. Her discontent with what God had allowed in her life turned to bitterness as seen by her response when they entered Bethlehem. The women there excitedly asked: *Can this be Naomi?* (Ruth 1:19). Naomi responded: *Don't call me Naomi. Call me Mara, because the Almighty has made my life very bitter. I went away full, but the Lord has brought me back empty. Why call me Naomi? The Lord has afflicted me; the Almighty has brought misfortune upon me* (Ruth 1:20-21).

Naomi chose for herself a name which meant bitter during this season of her life where she was overshadowed with sorrow, rather than choosing to maintain an attitude of joy (the name Naomi means "my joy"). Naomi failed to understand the character of God in the midst of her loss. Had she understood God had an eternal purpose for her life, she could have maintained her joy through these circumstances while she waited for God's plan to unfold.

God came through with His plan and the purpose was revealed in His bringing Naomi and Ruth to Bethlehem. Ruth began to work as a gleaner in the barley fields of a relative of Naomi's named Boaz. Boaz eventually took Ruth as his wife. A child, Obed, was born to Ruth and Naomi had the joy of caring for him. Naomi's joy was restored because of her daughter-in-law's faithfulness to what God had put before her—her mother-in-law. The women said to Naomi, *Praise be to the Lord, who this day has not left you without a kinsman-redeemer. May he become famous throughout Israel! He will renew your life and sustain you in your old age. For your daughter-in-law, who loves you and who is better to you than seven sons, has given him birth* (Ruth 4:14-15).

Obed became the father of Jesse, and Jesse the father of King David. What an awesome God! What Naomi and Ruth didn't know, is how God has honored them with the family heritage of being in the lineage of Jesus Christ! They didn't know how their life story would serve to encourage so many others in the years to come. We can maintain our joy in every circumstance, knowing that God is in control and has a purpose for all He allows into our lives. We can know that although we may not see or understand, God is sovereign, and what He is doing in our personal lives plays into His eternal plan, not just for our present-day, earthly lives, but for the lives of many others as well.

Joy comes from a spirit of celebration from deep within us as seen in the Apostle Paul's life in the book of Philippians. The four short chapters in this book changed my life as I captured the principles of Paul's inward joy.

My discontented, complaining thoughts disappeared as I meditated on Paul's attitude and the source of it. As you study this book, you will find that Paul was beaten and in prison, with the possibility of being beheaded overshadowing many of his days; yet, he freely ministered and wrote with joy, content in his situation. I had to ask, how? How could he continue on with his work in the midst of those extremely difficult circumstances? How could he hold onto his faith? He was able, due to the object of his focus. His focus was solely on Christ. In fact, Christ was his purpose for life! This is an important message for all Christians, but I think it is particularly important for those who are ministering on the front lines. It has helped me in times that I began to grow weary in well-doing. We continue forward with joy, not necessarily because we are appreciated by the people we serve, but because it is Christ who is the object of why we do what we do.

Paul lived with joy in his life despite his past and present circumstances. The fact that his past was spotted with the sin of persecuting Christians, even unto death, would have caused most Christians to believe God could not use them. But Paul lived his life with Christ as his purpose. What have you done in your life that has held you back from living for Christ. Most likely, you haven't been instrumental in killing God's people! Look at Philippians 3:13-14, *Brothers, I do not consider myself yet to have taken hold of it. But one thing I do: Forgetting what is behind and straining toward what is ahead, I press on toward the goal to win the prize for which God has called me heavenward in Christ Jesus.* For Paul, the secret to overcoming discontentment was to focus His attention on Christ and the purpose of God for his life. There was nothing he could do about the past, so he did not let himself become concerned about that. Rather, Paul focused on what God was calling him to do at the moment so that he would fulfill the purposes of God in the future.

Does a past failure haunt you? Have you made a bad choice or decision that forces you to live with consequences today? Has someone hurt you? Do not allow these things to become the object of your focus. Are these the things that occupy your thoughts? Only God deserves that kind of attention. We need to leave our past behind, as did Paul, and live with forward-vision. Ask Him to help you move forward, refocused on Christ.

As I write this book, I could focus on a person who tried to defame my character and harm my reputation with a professional group I am involved in. This lady wanted to do something I was already doing but in her twisted mind, she thought it was important that others thought it was her original idea. Therefore, in an attempt to build herself up, she lied and her lies could have been hurtful to my reputation. In the end, God exposed the lies and revealed the truth and all was well. I had to be intentional to not allow my mind to wander to her for long. I knew to have peace, I must focus on God. As I did that, I was led by His voice and able to do what He desired for me to do each day. God fulfills His purposes in our battles.

You must do the same. Be careful not to allow past and present circumstances to distract you from what God has for you to do now. The enemy is good at using distractions to capture our attention and pull our focus off God. God says that the battle is His and should not, therefore, be taking up our energy. Our energies need to be poured out on and for Christ.

Years ago, my husband abandoned me and left me with two children. At the time, I was equipped with only a high school diploma. I was faced with many trials in my attempts to survive and provide for us. Eventually God gave me an idea for a business. Started on a shoestring, He quickly prospered the business to three store locations where I earned a six-figure annual income.

In addition to God providing monetarily through that business, I met my husband, who I now co-labor with for the Lord. All the things that happened prior to this that were so devastating to me, that hurt me so tremendously, were used to refine me and bring me closer to God, preparing me for my future destiny. I think it is important to know that even the painful events in our lives can be used by God as stepping stones to the God-ordained place He desires to move us to. Now I am able to comfort others who experience similar afflictions and obstacles in their race and bring them hope for their future. Second Corinthians 1:4: *Who comforts (consoles and encourages) us in every trouble (calamity and affliction), so that we may also be able to comfort (console and encourage) those who are in any kind of trouble or distress, with the comfort (consolation and encouragement) with which we ourselves are comforted (consoled and encouraged) by God.*

Rejoicing in the midst of difficult circumstances doesn't mean you like them. When ill, we don't need to say, "Praise God I am so happy I am sick." What we might say instead is something like, "Praise God, although I am suffering He is with me and I am confident He will bring me through. My God is good and my healing is found in Christ. I will praise Him!"

Jesus didn't like the idea of having to suffer on the cross to redeem us. Look at what He said in the Garden of Gethsemane. He cried out to God the Father asking if there was any other way to accomplish His purpose. His anxiety was so deep that He sweat blood! That is intense! God sent angels to minister to Him and strengthen Him for His task (Luke 22:43-44).

Jesus went to the cross willingly, strengthened by the knowledge there was purpose in His suffering. But just as we would, if there could have been another way, He would have welcomed it. Yet, He surrendered to the Father's sovereign wisdom and said: *Nonetheless, not my will but yours be done.* Shouldn't we follow His example?

When I was struck with an illness that caused my wrists, elbows, knees and ankles to stiffen to the point where I could barely bend them and I was experiencing excruciating pain, believe me, I was not happy about the condition. I would pray and sometimes I would cry. Yet, I was able to maintain an inner joy in this situation because of my hope in Christ. I believed in His healing power. I believed that He had called me into ministry and to do things that would require me to be healed. I believed He would be faithful to His Word. I believed He had a purpose in the trial and it was for good and not to harm me (Jeremiah 29:11). I believed that by His grace I could handle and do anything because He would give me the strength for what He required of me. I believed that He would work it all out for good according to His purpose and plan. Just as Joseph held onto the visions God had given Him of his future, I held onto a Word God had spoken to me in my spirit, concerning His plan for me in ministering to His people. When God has given you a vision or a Word, and sudden circumstances don't fit it, hang on! God can change those circumstances just as sudden as they became what they are.

As it turns out, I spent my days watching recorded videos of old Oral Roberts healing crusades. At night I would go to sleep listening to recordings of Scripture promises for healing. I gained a deeper understanding concerning God's healing power. I grew in relationship with Christ and learned more about our life's purpose. Our life is not about us, it is all about God and His glory. I had been taught that humans were the center of everything and that God had created it all for us. But God taught me during this time that He was to be at the center of my life and that all of creation was created to magnify His glory. My faith in God increased. God became the object of my faith replacing my faith and desire to be healed, as the object of my faith. My faith in God grew to the point that I was comfortable to accept whatever His plan was. My confidence was in Him and His decision for me, realizing I may not understand it. One morning I awoke from sleep and found myself healed. My husband and I rejoiced in God's goodness toward us! Again, God has turned this into a testimony of His glory and I use it to comfort others who are hurting and to strengthen them with the hope we have in Christ.

I now realize that a person can have great faith in God and still not see their request granted this side of heaven. Real faith requires trusting God and His decision even when it does not line up with our idea of what is needed. It is not about getting what we want, but accepting what God does and does not do according to His wisdom and counsel, believing He has a good purpose in it. I have seen so many people hurt by wrong teachings about faith. Teachings that claimed a person had lack of faith because their loved one failed to receive their healing this side of heaven. I have seen no where in the Bible where it says that I can hold a person's life in my hands according to the amount of faith I have. It does say, however, the number of our days are held in God's hands. God alone is in control. We pray to God as the object of our faith, making our requests known, yet trusting He will answer the prayer according to His good purpose and eternal plan.

Again, let's consider Joseph's story in the Book of Genesis. Joseph's life was filled with betrayal from those whom he loved and who should have loved him. His brothers sold him into slavery. Imagine that! I am sure his heart was broken! Next, He faced false allegations from his master's wife. This resulted in his being thrown into prison. Yet, during his time in prison he conducted himself in a manner that drew people to him. He helped others, including helping to free one man who was wrongly imprisoned. He was faithful to do and be his best in the situation God had allowed in his life. He maintained his faith in God and held to the promise of God as given to him in a dream. Unknown to Joseph, God was using this time to refine him and prepare him for the position of authority that lied in his future. Eventually, Joseph realized his earlier dream and found himself the number two person in all of Egypt. He discovered that what had been meant for evil, God intended for good (Genesis 50:20). God had positioned him to save all of Israel. Only God could have known. It may be that only God knows the benefit(s) to be reaped from your painful situations. But, you can know you can trust Him.

Perhaps you have found yourself in situations where false allegations were made against you as did Paul and Joseph. It is a difficult place to be. You know you are innocent but those around you don't. False allegations can cause us to feel as though we have been put in a prison with no way out. Just as God opened that prison door for Joseph, just as He has done it for me, He will do it for you. He will make a way where there seems to be no way.

> *Forget the former things;*
> *do not dwell on the past.*
>
> *See, I am doing a new thing!*
> *Now it springs up; do you not perceive it?*
> *I am making a way in the desert*
> *and streams in the wasteland.*
>
> *The wild animals honor me, the jackals and the owls,*
> *because I provide water in the desert*
> *and streams in the wasteland,*
> *to give drink to my people, my chosen*
>
> *the people I formed for myself*
> *that they may proclaim my praise*
>
> (Isaiah 43:18-21 NIV).

Maintaining satisfaction through difficult times is dependent on our level of trust in the character of God. When we trust God, we know that everything He allows in our lives has a purpose whether we know what the purpose is or not. Jeremiah 29:11: *'For I know the plans I have for you,'* declares the Lord, *'plans to prosper you and not to harm you, plans to give you hope and a future.'* Many times God uses our trials to teach, mold, and perfect us (James 1:2-4). Many times they come right before a promotion whether it be in our spiritual walk, ministry or another area of our life.

In 2 Kings 6, we read about the story of Elisha and his servant when approaching the battle between King Aram and Israel. In verse seventeen, Elisha prays, *O Lord, open his eyes so he may see.* The story goes on to say that God did open his eyes and he was able to see the heavenly armies ready to do battle for Israel. These armies could not be seen by the naked eye. Sometimes when I find myself in a challenging situation I ask God to open my eyes to see what is going on. I ask Him to give me His eternal perspective in it. Sometimes He does and sometimes He doesn't. Either way, I know there is no need to be dismayed because the LORD God is with me wherever I go (Joshua 1:9). I know He will bring me through, and that His purpose is being worked out through it all. I know this because I know the character of God. I know that He is faithful to His Word. He is not a man who lies. I know His love has been proven in Christ Jesus.

Life may spin out of control and everything in it may fail you, but you can be content because God is your source for everything you need. He is your strength for the situation. Maintain trust and hope in the Lord and it will transform your fear of the future into a desire to rejoice in God just as Habakkuk's trust did in Habakkuk 3:17-19. He says:

> *Though the fig tree does not bud*
> *and there are no grapes on the vines,*
> *though the olive crop fails*
> *and the fields produce no food,*
> *though there are no sheep in the pen*
> *and no cattle in the stalls,*
> *yet I will rejoice in the Lord,*
> *I will be joyful in God my Savior.*

Don't be distracted by your circumstances. Have faith in God; and like Ruth, do those things you know to do today. Be faithful to the assignment

God has given you for this season. Like Joseph, help others wherever God has you for the moment. With joy watch God fulfill His plan through the circumstances of your life, just as you have seen Him do in the past in your life and the lives of others. God will be your strength enabling you to walk through just as the Apostle Paul proclaimed He was for him and prayed he would be for others. Ephesians 3:16: I *pray that out of his glorious riches he may strengthen you with power through his Spirit in your inner being.* This same strength is available to you and me.

James 2:26 says: *For as the body without the spirit is dead, so faith without works is dead also.* It is your faith in God revealed in your actions that empowers you to live a life of joy and satisfaction. Let go of the past and focus on where God is taking you. Realize He is working out His plan for your life. Focus on what He is calling you to do in today's circumstances that will enable you to walk into the purpose God has for your future. Lean on Him and walk through your circumstances, not in your own strength, but in His.

Christ prepared His disciples with the knowledge that they would sometimes experience pruning by God, the vinedresser (John 15:1-11). When I picture pruning shears, I immediately imagine some pain. Sometimes we find ourselves in hurtful situations but it helps us to persevere knowing there is purpose in them. We are to keep the faith, remain in Christ and pray for His will to be done in our lives. When faced with challenges, the first thing I do is ask God, "What are you desiring to do in me through this situation, Lord?" God does not put or allow any situation in our lives that He doesn't have a purpose to use for our good, or for someone else's good. He has a "big picture" perspective; whereas, we have a "small picture" perspective concerning the affairs of life, so we need to trust God in them. As we do, we will bear good fruit, and our lives will glorify God.

No matter what the situation is, we can remain content in it because we know God is working out His plan. In Psalm 16:11, we are told we can have fullness of joy in our circumstances, because we belong to God. Christians can be free from living discontented, unfulfilled, joyless lives. God will equip His children to receive genuine joy and satisfaction in the place of discontent, greed, covetousness and depression as we put our faith in Him.

Moments at the Fountain

Reflection & Application

Things to Remember

- The restless heart is satisfied through rejoicing in what the Lord has done, is doing and will do. It rests in the character of God and the eternal hope found in Christ.

- Life may spin out of control but you can be satisfied knowing God is your strength and deliverer.

- Trusting and hoping in the Lord, and the promises we have in Him, transforms fear of the future into a desire to rejoice.

- You can be satisfied in every situation knowing God is in control and will bring purpose out of it.

Jeremiah 29:11

'For I know the plans I have for you,' declares the Lord, 'plans to prosper you and not to harm you, plans to give you hope and a future.'

Isaiah 43:19

Behold, I will do something new, Now it will spring forth;
Will you not be aware of it?
I will even make a roadway in the wilderness,
Rivers in the desert.

Luke 22:42

Saying, "Father, if You are willing, remove this cup from Me; yet not My will, but Yours be done."

Habakkuk 3:17-19 (MSG)

> ...Though the sheep pens are sheepless
> and the cattle barns empty,
> I'm singing joyful praise to God.
> I'm turning cartwheels of joy to my Savior God.
> Counting on God's Rule to prevail,
> I take heart and gain strength...

Nehemiah 8:9-10 (MSG)

> ...Don't weep and carry on. "...Don't feel bad. The joy of
> GOD is your strength!"

Habakkuk 3:17 (AMP)

> Yet I will rejoice in the Lord; I will exult in the [victorious]
> God of my salvation!

Psalm 13:5

> But I trust in your unfailing love; my heart rejoices in your
> salvation.

Reflect & Grow

1. What past failures or hurts are you still focusing on? How has that robbed you of joy? What can you refocus your attention to in order to find healing?

2. Consider the account in Nehemiah 8, especially verses 9-12. What instruction was given to the Israelites concerning weeping over their sin? Why were they told they should rejoice? Why is it you can rejoice—what provision has been made for your sin? Does accepting this truth bring healing to your soul?

3. Do you find yourself reflecting on a good or negative heritage? What is the problem with that? If the past is positive, is it still a problem to focus on it? Why or why not?

4. What does Jeremiah 29:11 tell us about God's plans for us?

5. How is your faith in God being revealed in your life? In good times? In challenging times?

6. How might a knowledge and acceptance of Hebrews 13:8 help you trust God?

7. Do you think Jesus was happy about enduring the cross? How was He able to stay satisfied when looking ahead to the cross? Can you apply this attitude to your own situations? How?

8. What does James 1:2-4 describe as a benefit of our trials?

9. Make a list of some of the difficult times you have had. Now ask the Holy Spirit to reveal to you the purpose? Was there something you were to learn? Did you grow closer to God? Did it change your perspective on life, God, or others? Was someone else encouraged by your steadfast faith in God despite your circumstances?

10. What was Jesus' joy? What did He mean that He wanted His joy to remain in His disciples (us)? See John 17:13.

11. Name at least three things that have been mentioned in this chapter that help us rejoice and endure trying times.

12. What can we do to make the desire Jesus had for us in John 15:11 a reality in our lives? Read 1 Thessalonians 5:16-22.

Prayer

Father, thank You that I can maintain my joy in every circumstance knowing that You are in control and have purpose for anything and everything You allow in my life. Just as Your grace was sufficient for Paul when he prayed for the thorn in his flesh to be removed, Your grace is sufficient for me. I rejoice in Your plans for me, knowing they are good and not intended to harm me. I look forward to the joy that will overflow as a result of their fulfillment.

Confession

I trust in the character of God and know that He will work all things together for good in my life. I know His plan is good according to Jeremiah 29:11. I am God's workmanship, becoming more like Christ every day.

Chapter 7 ——————————————————————

Living Committed

*I press on toward the goal to win the prize for which
God has called me heavenward in Christ Jesus.*

Philippians 3:14

*H*ave you ever looked at life and thought about how little control you hold over your circumstances? Think about it: Did you have any control concerning the time of your birth? Where you were born? Who your parents are? What body shape, eye color, or skin color you were born with? Think about your growing-up years: Did you choose the school you attended? Where you lived? How your family celebrated holidays? How your mother and/or father parented you? How about your present circumstances – How much control do you have over them? Can you control the weather – when it will rain or the sun will shine? Can you force those who are in your life to treat you right or to do what is right in the situations of life? What kind of control do you have over the politics at your church or work place? Hopefully, you are not like my brother who found himself out of work when the factory he had worked at for seventeen years, suddenly closed. How much control do you really have over your circumstances?

The reality is that there are many circumstances that you have absolutely *no* control over. Therefore, it is impossible to live satisfied if you are depending on ideal circumstances to do so. While ideal circumstances present themselves on occasion, for the most part, we are faced with changes and circumstances that are beyond our control.

Paul recognized he was not in control of his circumstances, but he knew someone who was. He discovered the secret of joy and satisfaction was not to depend on his circumstances but to depend on Christ who would supply all his needs (Philippians 4:19), including the strength for trying situations. Paul was also content, no matter what his circumstances, because Jesus' glory was his priority. He said in Philippians 1:21, ...*To live is Christ and to die is gain.* Without a commitment to Christ — without choosing to believe, receive, and obey what God says and allows as a sovereign God, your circumstances will deprive you of satisfaction.

Paul believed and lived out the truth that nothing compares to the promise we have in Christ Jesus. Therefore, his focus was on eternity. Philippians 3:8 says: *What is more, I consider everything a loss compared to the surpassing greatness of knowing Christ Jesus my Lord, for whose sake I have lost all things. I consider them rubbish that I may gain Christ.*

Because he made a decision to live for Christ and to accept what Jesus said as truth, Paul kept his eyes on the Lord and the eternal promises Jesus had shown him. This commitment enabled Paul to tap into the power of God so that he experienced beatings, stoning, jailing, shipwreck, hunger, desertion, misunderstanding and more without losing his joy.

Paul's commitment to Christ did not wane, even when it appeared his ministry goals were not going to happen. For example, Paul desired to preach in Rome, yet was imprisoned, unable to preach publicly. Even worse, he faced the possibility of beheading! Yet, he ministered to those who were around him, completely content. He wrote a letter to the Philippians, proclaiming acceptance of the circumstances God had placed him in. Paul was not complaining. He was joyful and satisfied with his life, even while in prison, not knowing if he would realize his dream.

Some prisons don't have bars and locked doors. For example, perhaps you are in a job where you feel trapped or a marriage that is on the rocks. You feel like running away. Could it be that God has a mission for you in the place He has you? Or, perhaps God has you there to refine and perfect you. Many times we fail to thank God for His provision while we pray and wait for God to open doors or change our relationships. We can ask God for His strength, favor and wisdom to stand in His perfect will, whatever that might be. When it comes to marriages, I will have to say, many times people flee their marriage too easily, saying, "God doesn't want me to be miserable." They may even run into the imprisonment of another similar relationship. Sometimes, our focus is mistakenly on finding happiness instead of on seeking Christ, where happiness exists. Ultimately, God is more concerned about our holiness than our happiness.[16] Yet, God knows that when we pursue holiness, we will find happiness. Happiness is experienced as a by-product of an intimate relationship with God.

If you are a woman who finds herself in an abusive environment, however, I am not advocating you stay there. Instead, you should find somewhere to stay that is safe and pray for God to move on the heart of your husband to get help. God does not expect you to be beaten or to live where your life is in danger. On the other hand, guard yourself from running away from a marriage just because you don't have things your way. The marriage relationship provides a perfect environment for God to do His work of refinement. Sometimes our work places provide such an opportunity as well. A heart pursuing God will often say, "God, give me your strength and wisdom for my situation," or, "God, change me and use me in my spouse's life or in this job according to your will and purpose." Romans 5:3-5, speaking of our trials, informs us: *And not only this, but we also exult in our tribulations, knowing that tribulation brings about perseverance; and perseverance, proven character; and proven character, hope; and hope does not disappoint, because the love of God has been poured out within our hearts through the Holy Spirit who was given to us.* First Peter 1:6-7 says: *In this you greatly rejoice, though now for a little while you may have had to suffer grief in all kinds of trials. These have come so that your faith—of greater worth than gold, which perishes even though refined by fire—may be proved genuine and may result in praise, glory and honor when Jesus Christ is revealed.* Our hope for happiness, our hope for transformation, our hope for anything and everything good is in Christ. Romans 5:5 and 12:12 encourages us that our hope will not disappoint us.

One day, I found myself faced with the challenge of raising two young teenagers alone. This was not my decision. We were abandoned and left in quite a pickle financially. I did not choose it for my life. I dreamed of the perfect marriage, perfect family and living happily ever after as a wife and mother. I know some of you have had the same dream, only to experience its death. Here I was in a circumstance out of my control – beyond my ability to change, and my dream was gone.

Although I had no power over the circumstance itself, I did have the power to choose how I would respond to it. I could focus on what I had lost. I could stay in utter depression, consider myself a failure, be miserable the rest of my life, and set an example to my children of quitting on life, crying while singing the song "woe is me." That certainly was one option. Or, I could focus on what I had not lost – my children, my God and my faith in God. I could pick myself up and hit the road to find a job that would provide for us. After a short time of grieving my loss, I chose the second option.

I began a job search only to find that my qualifications, which at that time consisted of a high school education, did not qualify me for a job that would pay enough to support us sufficiently. After much prayer and perseverance, God eventually gave me a business idea that brought in thousands of dollars a month. My children were raised with an attitude that all things work together to their good as they trust in God. They witnessed what it means to overcome even in the midst of what most people would consider very unfavorable circumstances. Praise be to God!

The only way we can truly handle the extreme difficulties of life and maintain satisfaction is by having a life committed to Christ. When we learn to live committed to Christ, as did Paul, everything pales in comparison. Christ was Paul's life. Paul was surrendered to Him in mind and body. He fully trusted God's plan for his life. Paul commented that he had only one desire and that was that Christ be exalted in his body, whether by life or by death. His attitude was: "Lord, whatever you want to do with me, I surrender to it. I know you have a purpose and I am committed to you and your purpose. I give my life to you as a living sacrifice to do with it what you please. If I live, praise the Lord. If I die, praise the Lord." His only desire was that Christ be glorified through his life. When we are committed to Christ to this degree, nothing will have enough power or influence to rob us of our satisfaction. So, Paul was able to accept his circumstances with contentment because he knew God — His character and His ways — therefore, he knew he could trust God no matter what. He knew Jesus had conquered hell, death and the grave. Therefore, he had no fear of death. Knowing he would be with the Lord, should he die, enabled him to say it would be a benefit to die. He only desired to stay alive to finish the work Christ had given Him. He hoped to complete His assignment and help to fully equip the believers he would be leaving behind with a firm knowledge of God and the gospel of Christ.

Before Jon and I received the call to prepare for vocational ministry, we were favored with material things, able to purchase or do most anything we could want. We were blessed and we were satisfied physically, materially and spiritually. However, shortly after selling our business in obedience to the Lord, we entered a season of trial and temptation. Life-threatening and debilitating illnesses struck both my parents and me, all in the same year. Finances dwindled away to nothing, and material possessions were lost. That was the trial. The temptation was to believe the lie Satan was feeding us that God's Word is not true – that we should turn away from Him and abandon the path He had set us on. In fact, if we looked at our new circumstances, it did not make sense to believe we would be able to complete ministry training, let alone have finances for full-time ministry. It seemed foolish to think anyone could believe in us enough to sponsor us to plant and pastor a church. Our circumstances had changed drastically, but we chose to reject the lie of Satan and continue trusting God.

Suffering a financial crisis followed by a health crisis, we experienced what it means to walk by faith versus sight. Did fear and disappointment try to overtake us? Of course, it did. We cried and we prayed. But we chose to believe God's Word and trust His faithfulness, no matter what. The Bible says although sorrow may come for the night, joy will come in the morning. We knew God had given us a Word and that He would be faithful to fulfill it. Therefore, turning back or quitting were not options in our minds. We set our eyes on Christ and we walked through the hard time doing those things we knew to do day by day, with an expectation of receiving the reward Christ promised us for believing Him.

The Christian walk is indeed a walk of faith and not of sight. We need to order our lives according to our faith in God and His character, not according to what we see in our circumstances. Take Christian inspirational speaker and author, Joni Erickson Tada's circumstances, for example. She is in a kind of prison because of the condition of her body. She became paralyzed from the neck down after a diving accident as a teenager. But Joni has joy despite her physical circumstances. How can she be satisfied with her life with these conditions? Her joy certainly does not come by choosing to fight against Christ! Rather, Joni has chosen to surrender to what God has allowed to happen in her life. She looks forward to the day when she will see Jesus face to face, but until then she is content to glorify God through her paralysis.

We need to understand that we can be content in spite of painful and trying experiences. We can cry tears of sadness and grief and know deep peace and satisfaction at the same time. It is truly a supernatural thing. It is possible to have a deep, abiding spiritual satisfaction that never leaves us simply because of our trust in God. Trust deepens as we cultivate a surrendered and committed heart toward Christ and allow Him to be Lord of our present and future circumstances. We also need to commit to the study of His Word. Without that, we will not be able to keep our focus on Jesus.

We experience satisfaction as we accept Christ's sovereignty and turn the control of our lives over to Him. We make a conscious decision to make Christ the goal of our lives, refusing to allow circumstances to deprive us of our joy. When we remember that following the impulses from our flesh will result in a loss when we stand before God, whereas, following Christ has eternal rewards, we are encouraged on our journey. In Matthew 19:27-29 Peter and Jesus are talking: *Peter answered him, 'We have left everything to follow you! What then will there be for us?' Jesus said to them, 'I tell you the truth, at the renewal of all things, when the Son of Man sits on his glorious throne, you who have followed me will also sit on twelve thrones, judging the twelve tribes of Israel. And everyone who has left houses or brothers or sisters or father or mother or children or fields for my sake will receive a hundred times as much and will inherit eternal life.'*

As we walk through the circumstances of life hand in hand with Jesus, we realize He is faithful. We can feel secure to commit our lives to Him.

Moments at the Fountain

Reflection & Application

Things to Remember

- The restless become satisfied by surrendering their own will and committing to Christ and His will for their life.

- It is a supernatural thing to be content in the midst of sadness and grief.

- We experience satisfaction as we accept Christ's sovereignty in our lives and surrender to His Lordship over our past, present and future circumstances.

- We experience the reality of our faith in the difficult times of life.

- We can be satisfied as we invoke the power given us to choose a biblical response to life's circumstances.

Jeremiah 29:11 (MSG)
I know what I'm doing. I have it all planned out—plans to take care of you, not abandon you, plans to give you the future you hope for.

Romans 12:12 (NLT)
Rejoice in our confident hope. Be patient in trouble, and keep on praying.

Philippians 1:21

For to me, to live is Christ and to die is gain.

Philippians 3:8

What is more, I consider everything a loss because of the surpassing worth of knowing Christ Jesus my Lord, for whose sake I have lost all things. I consider them garbage, that I may gain Christ.

Matthew 19:29

And everyone who has left houses or brothers or sisters or father or mother or wife or children or fields for my sake will receive a hundred times as much and will inherit eternal life.

Reflect & Grow

1. What does Christ promise us in John 16:33?

2. Why can we be of good cheer in our trials according to Jesus in the above verse? Also see Romans 8:28-29.

3. Life will have its difficult times. Job found himself in a season of loss, pain and trauma. Read Job 2:7-10. How did Job respond? What do you learn from this story?

4. What are you most committed to in life? Career? Ministry? Children? Who or what has first place in your life? If any person, including your spouse, is at the center of your life, what will happen when they let you down or fail to measure up to your expectations?

5. What needs to change in your life so you can testify Christ is Lord of it?

6. What does a walk of faith look like? Do those with faith have a life free of trials and pain?

7. If your prayers are not answered as you hoped, does that mean you lack faith? Explain.

8. Do you feel the need to control? What areas of your life, if any, are you having difficulty surrendering to God's care? Your children, husband, job, parents, betrayal, finances, etc? What could be hindering your release of these things to Christ?

9. Why is God more concerned about your holiness than your happiness?

10. Why must you learn about the character of God and His ways to experience satisfaction while on your life's journey?

11. Who does have the control of the affairs of our lives? Read Isaiah 44:24. How does this make you feel?

12. Read Matthew 19:29, Philippians 3 and Daniel 6 for examples of faithfulness to God. How about you – are you willing to follow Christ at any cost? Consider and discuss.

Prayer

Father, You control the clouds and make the lightning flash. You hold the number of my days in Your hands and my destiny in Your heart. Thank you, that by Your grace, I am able to surrender to Your plans and commit to Your ways. Help me, Lord, to continually trust in You. Help me to follow Your lead. Thank You for flooding me with a peace that passes understanding and a love that satisfies my soul. I commit my life to You and ask for Your grace and boldness to stand, no matter what circumstance I might face. In Jesus' name, I pray.

Confession

Like Paul, I consider all things a loss compared to the surpassing greatness of knowing Christ. I consider it all rubbish – the great things and the trials – that I may gain Christ. I commit my life to Him.

Chapter 8 ———————————————————

Loving People

What causes fights and quarrels among you?
Don't they come from your desires that battle within you?
You want something but don't get it. You kill and covet,
but you cannot have what you want. You quarrel and fight.
You do not have, because you do not ask God.

James 4:1-2

At times, we let the actions of others rob us of our satisfaction. I have discovered that we set ourselves up for this when we put our expectations on people – when we expect people to act, react, respond, think or do what we think they should do, and to be what we think they should be. Our own unrealistic expectations can set us up for disappointment and lead to dissatisfaction.

I have always been a people lover. I was voted most congenial in school and always stood up for the less fortunate when others persecuted them unfairly. I still love people today, especially those in the family of God. Yet, there are times when I assume someone should respond or think as I do about a situation. This really does show my prideful nature. Why should everyone be like me? Am I the perfect one? Of course not. When I do this, I find myself disappointed. Perhaps you can relate. We should be careful not to project our aspirations on those around us.

Before entering into vocational ministry, I had my own business and employed people. You can believe I had ample opportunity to lose my joy and satisfaction. In fact, I did lose it because at that time I did not understand this principle of not putting my expectations on others, allowing them to be who God created them to be. I expected people to have the same work ethics I had always had and to respond to their boss the way I had always responded to mine. Don't get me wrong. I do believe people should be held to some ethical work standards and accountable for their actions. However, we also have to remember that we all have different backgrounds and perspectives; and as Christians, we are in different stages of our spiritual walk. We are God's workmanship and He has to complete that work. He may have done some extensive refining in one area of an individual's life, yet another area is less refined; whereas, He may be working in the opposite order with us.

If you are in church, you know that everyone in the church has not necessarily discovered that it is to their best interest to make Christ and the advancement of His Kingdom their focus. Some in the church still have their focus on what it is they can get out of the church, instead of what they can bring to it. Without Christ being their priority, their spiritual maturity may be that of an infant, even though they may have been in church for several years.

In addition, the universal church has many wounded souls whom God is healing and sanctifying. Sometimes during this process people are focused on the wrong things. They may be focused on themselves, which often results in being easily offended. They may be focused on their own desires, and some may have trouble submitting to the decisions of leadership when it is not the decision they hoped for. The truth is, we are all born into this world self-centered, and we find many are still looking for satisfaction in all the wrong places, in all the wrong ways, according to their different degrees of self-centeredness. Speaking of spiritual immaturity and self centeredness in the church, James 4:1-2 puts it like this, *What causes fights and quarrels among you? Don't they come from your desires that battle within you? You want something but don't get it. You kill and covet, but you cannot have what you want. You quarrel and fight. You do not have, because you do not ask God.*

I have heard several un-churched people call those in the church hypocrites. It is not that we are hypocrites so much as we are still in process.

We realize we cannot save ourselves and we need a Savior. We have a relationship with Christ but the level of relationship varies from person to person. We are saved, but our minds have yet to be fully renewed and the transformation has not yet fully taken place within us. Our spirits were born again, but our minds were not.

Our minds still have to be brought into alignment with the Word of God, and that takes a willingness and effort on the part of each individual. Some submit to the process more quickly than others. Romans 7:24-25 says: *What a wretched man I am! Who will rescue me from this body of death? Thanks be to God—through Jesus Christ our Lord! So then, I myself in my mind am a slave to God's law, but in the sinful nature a slave to the law of sin.* This Scripture says that I serve God in my spirit but my body is controlled by my thoughts which have not yet come into complete agreement with the Word of God. In order for my actions to line up with God's ways, my thinking has to be transformed, and that is a process. It doesn't happen overnight even for those who are diligently seeking God and spending time in His Word. And those who are not, they are what the Bible calls carnal Christians. If they are still living life out of their old nature instead of as the new creation they are in Christ, we most definitely cannot expect actions that reflect spiritual maturity. God has to bring them to a place where they desire to have a change inwardly and grow in His ways outwardly.

As we grow spiritually, we learn to forgive. Our focus is not to have our own way or to prove ourselves right. It is on what God desires – reconciliation, maintaining unity, and pressing onward with our mission as the body of Christ. In addition, because of insecurities, past emotional wounds, low self-esteem, and other unresolved soul issues, many Christians continue to make poor choices in their lives and demonstrate behavior that is not appropriate for a person who is aspiring to be like Christ.

The depth of the hunger you have for Christ plus the amount of time spent reading and studying His word will determine where you are in the sanctification process. Those who choose to put on the mind of Christ, by coming into agreement with what the Bible says, will be stable in their faith no matter what people or circumstances they encounter in their lives. They learn to apply Philippians 4:8 to their situations involving people: *Finally, brothers, whatever is true, whatever is noble, whatever is right, whatever is pure, whatever is lovely, whatever is admirable—if anything is excellent or praiseworthy—think about such things.*

If a Christian has not progressed very far in the process of sanctification, no matter how many years they have been saved, then they may still be walking, living, and reacting according to their old, pre-salvation mindset. They may be stuck in old habit patterns that create pain for themselves and others. They may conform outwardly; however, without inward change, outward conformity will soon break down. But be of good cheer. God has promised to perfect us all, and He will be faithful to complete what He has started in each one of us. The process will not be complete until we meet Him face to face. Meanwhile, those who are not submitted are responding to their emotions and old nature's mindset. They cannot understand the righteous actions of someone who is submitted to God and, consequently, walking on a different spiritual plain. Therefore, until we stand before Christ, purpose in your heart to give people lots of grace in place of your expectations. This way, you will not be robbed of your joy, and your satisfaction in life will remain intact. You can allow others to be who God has made them to be. Wait patiently for Him to perfect them in His time and in His way (Philippians 1:6). Besides, at times, you need others to do the same for you.

As I write this, my mind drifts back to a time when my husband and I returned to the states from a trip to the GCI Missions School in Romania. We landed in Italy and boarded a jet headed to New York City. As we taxied to the runway, we suddenly heard the pilot's voice come over the speakers. He told us that we were taxiing off the runway due to a discovered malfunction with the aircraft. I praised the Lord. Thank God they discovered the problem before we took off! Some people began complaining almost instantly, while others waited a while, but my mentality was, "Praise God! Whatever it takes to fix it, we want this plane fixed while we are still on the ground!"

After three hours of sitting on the plane, not in a more comfortable terminal, you can imagine the frustration everyone was feeling. When we finally got the green light from the mechanics, we took off for the long flight to New York. But, when we reached New York we discovered more problems. You probably guessed it – we had missed our connecting flight.

The gate attendant said she was not able to help us.

I questioned, "You mean you don't have procedures in place when this kind of thing happens?" I was sure we were not the first people to miss a connecting flight due to their plane being late. She called someone else over to help her. But they didn't know how to help us either. I was tired and it had been a long trip. Now they were telling me that we were stuck at the JFK airport in New York City. If they didn't know how to get us home, who did? I could feel my patience leaving and my temperature rising. Jon said, "Sarah, just be patient. Everything will be all right."

I had lost my satisfaction. But that was not the worst of it. They sent us on a trip across the airport. Have you been to the JFK airport? It is humongous. We pulled large suitcases for miles! We had to go outside, up and down hills, back inside, up in the elevator, on the train and finally we arrived at our destination. It seemed like we had traveled to another city! As we approached the counter, I said, "Hallelujah!" There was no line. We handed the attendant our tickets. We told her our dilemma and that the gate agent had directed us to her for help. However, the satisfaction of being able to walk straight up to the counter without waiting left abruptly as I heard her say, "Why did they send you to me? They are not supposed to do that. I am here all by myself. They need to take care of you down there!" I was angry and frustrated and I let this situation rob me of my contentment. I suddenly realized God was allowing this whole circumstance because He was after something in me. He wanted to develop patience in me when dealing with people, trusting His ability to work in, through and around them.

How about you? What's your response when another driver pulls out in front of you and you just miss him? Do you scream out at him, "You are not qualified to be behind the wheel of a car"? How about the cashier who is having a great time conversing with the customer in line in front of you while you are running late for a meeting? Does your emotional temperature rise to the point it is seen in your face color and actions? Or, how do you respond when you have an appointment with someone and they don't show or call until the scheduled time has come and gone?

God allows these incidents to happen in our lives to teach us about the need for grace toward others. God has taught me through these kinds of situations to stop being in such a hurry and just relax. As He has been patient with me, so He empowers me to be patient with others. Don't get me wrong, I am not saying I do this perfectly; but by the grace of God, I am getting better at it.

Think about your spouse... your children... your co-workers? Do you find yourself upset with them because you think they should be and do what you expect them to be or to do? For example, sometimes as parents we expect our three-year-old to behave as a five-year-old. We put our unrealistic expectations on them and find ourselves frustrated and angry, unable to enjoy our children. Every day, in all your relationships and in living out life, you have opportunities to put your expectations on others or to accept them as they are at this time. It is important to remember that everyone has a unique personality. They are not going to be just like you. How boring it would be if we were all the same.

Another painful event can be a friend's betrayal of your friendship. What are you going to do if you have a friend deceive you? Will you still maintain an attitude of satisfaction? I have had someone whom I thought was a close friend betray me. It was in a business deal. Her response was, "Don't take it personally, it is just business." I admit it took me a full year to completely rid my heart of unforgiveness. I went to God every time I realized it still existed, hidden in a crevice of my heart. I said, "God I do not want this to separate me from you. It is not worth it. I love you and I am thankful for your forgiveness towards me. Please help me to forgive." Finally, the day came when I could hear good reports about her life and I could genuinely be happy for her. My heart was finally free.

I remember when someone I admired and respected responded towards me with jealousy. Their unkind words spoken to another were brought to my attention. The whole incident left me questioning my value. Isn't it amazing that we turn to others to discover our worth – that we give them power to control joy and contentment in our lives? We allow their perspective, which is at least as limited and darkened as our own, to affect us in how we see ourselves. We allow their choices to affect us—thinking their choice to do evil against us has to do with some lack in us. Would it not be wiser instead to rely on God's unchanging and encouraging reassurance? I have decided that it is. I hope you will too.

God so loved us that He gave His Son for us. How significant we are! How valuable we are! The Creator of all that is has made us according to the counsel of His Will for His good pleasure and purpose. There is no greater source from which to receive our significance. He made us and He saw His creation was good! We can be satisfied knowing He has made us valuable.

Again, this hurtful event turned out for my good as it drove me to Christ and to discover my identity and value in Him. Maintaining satisfaction in dealing with people, or trying situations, makes us realize God's hand in the details of the affairs of our lives. He uses the events and people in our lives to mold and shape us into glorious vessels and to draw us closer to Him.

Through allowing God to forgive another through us (***it is no longer I who*** *live, but Christ* ***lives in me*** – Galatians 2:20), we can forgive quickly and, at times, immediately. Unfortunately, the forgiven party, many times, has difficulty believing they have been forgiven. They may continue to act in a defensive manner, thinking the other person still holds a grudge, even though they have grown passed it. This results in a split to continue, and many times to worsen, when it doesn't need to. I do want to point out however, that releasing forgiveness and trusting are different responses. Trust is earned or lost through a person's actions toward us. When trust is broken, it can take time for the abuser to earn our trust again. Whereas, forgiveness is a decision to release our control over another; releasing them to the only One who may rightfully judge. It is done by the grace of God.

When I think about Christ and how He must have felt when Judas betrayed Him, and how He must have felt when Peter denied Him, my heart weeps. But Jesus knew God was in control and it was part of God's plan. This brought Him strength to endure. Consider the ridicule and mocking from the soldiers and the people. Jesus asked the Father to forgive them. Although He experienced horrendous pain, He never lost the satisfaction of knowing that His life's purpose was playing out as He hung on that cross. Christ's mind was set on us, and His thoughts were on fulfilling the covenant made in heaven between He and Father God that guaranteed our salvation. His thoughts were on us – the reward of His suffering! How about you? Are your thoughts on God and things above, or are you more concerned about your earthly rewards than your eternal ones?

You have no control over others. They will make their decisions and you have no control over what they will do or how they will feel. Some will like you. Some will not. Some may even try to hurt you and falsely persecute you. They persecuted Jesus and they persecuted Paul. Why wouldn't you and I, as His followers, be persecuted too? It helps to remember that it is actually not a personal endeavor but it is the Christ in you that the spirit of this world persecutes. The anti-Christ spirit does his work through people, inside and outside of the church, though often they are oblivious to it.

The best way to prevent people's actions from affecting our emotions is to make Christ's mind our mind. In order to do this, you must know what Christ's mind is like. We find that description in Philippians 2:5-8: *Your attitude should be the same as that of Christ Jesus: Who, being in very nature God, did not consider equality with God something to be grasped, but made himself nothing, taking the very nature of a servant, being made in human likeness. And being found in appearance as a man, he humbled himself and became obedient to death—even death on a cross!* Jesus is God; yet, He took upon Himself the form of a servant and became a bondservant of love.

Paul identifies himself as a bondservant in the book of Philippians. The Greek word for bondservant is *doulos*. We find the characteristics of a bondservant described in Deuteronomy, chapter fifteen. Here, we read about the slave bought for a price, then freed by his master. Instead of taking freedom, the bondservant chose to remain a slave forever because he loved his master. By his own choice, he would serve his master's household for the rest of his life. The bondservant freely surrendered his will to his master. He trusted, instead, in his master's will for his life.

Paul said he too was bought with a price, but he was bound to Jesus by the bonds of love, not of duty or coercion. It was his desire that his will be consumed by his master's. It was his joy that Christ be exalted in his body. A bondservant does not focus on himself. His focus is on his master. A bondservant regards others more important than himself. In fact, when you have the attitude of a servant towards others you cease striving with them. They may strive with you, but you will do everything in your power to maintain peace with those around you. I am not talking about being a peacekeeper but a *peacemaker*.

A peacekeeper stuffs their feelings for a resemblance of peace, but that is not true peace, as a severe crack in the relationship exists. True peace is obtained when feelings are communicated. Seek peace by talking out misunderstandings. Give others the opportunity to explain their behaviors before you make conclusions.

Sometimes we discover we have wrong perceptions, or have misunderstood an action or intent behind someone's words. When both people are walking in the spirit of Christ, communication normally results in bringing true peace back into the relationship. But when not, you can rest knowing that you have done what God requires of you. You have sought to seek out truth and make peace, though they denied it. Your relationship with the Lord, therefore, is intact.

You may discover you are not able to walk in fellowship with this person any longer, if after talking it over, you see their motives were ungodly and they have no repentance for it. Again, you are free as you walk away from that relationship as you have done what is required of you before God. God does not expect us to be fools but to be wise.

Bondservants loved not only their masters but all those who were in their master's household. Likewise, bondservants of Jesus love other Christians simply because they belong to Christ. Matthew 10:24-25 says: *A student is not above his teacher, nor a servant above his master.* We are commanded to love others, and all of us have been given the ability by the grace of God to forgive others and love them even though they may have treated us unfairly. It is a choice. We do it because we love God and He has forgiven us. We do it because He continues to forgive us when we fail Him. We do it by allowing the love of God to flow through us. Should we have to disassociate with them, however, we can still love them from afar.

I can meet someone in the body of Christ and instantly form a bond with them, feeling as though I have known them for years. I truly feel a love for them. This is not natural for the unregenerate soul, but for the regenerate, it can be and most certainly should be as we grow in our relationship with Christ. It is not us, but the Spirit of Christ in us loving His people through us. Commit your will to Christ's and begin to love others in your Master's household simply because they belong to Him. It will change your life.

We should also apply the bondservant's way of love to our marriages. I have seen people leave their spouses, putting their own happiness above the happiness of their partner and children. Exalting oneself like this is in direct contrast to taking on the mind of a bondservant and regarding others more highly than ourselves.

Jesus was obedient to God. He was a bondservant. It cost Him His life. His love, shown in His laying down His life for us, resulted in our salvation. What might result from your sacrificial love shown towards your spouse or another in your sphere of influence? Only God knows. Yet, as we develop a servant's mind by putting on the mind of Christ, we know the supernatural satisfaction and peace that comes from putting others before ourselves.

Still, loving people is not the answer, in itself, to our satisfaction issues. If you are not married, do not let yourself fall into the trap of thinking that marriage will bring you fulfillment and satisfaction. The truth is, no human being, including a spouse, can fill the void that exists in your soul. If you get married in order to have your spiritual needs met, you will surely be disappointed. Don't misunderstand me. Marriage is a wonderful institution. In fact, God commands those who have a physical lust to seek a spouse and make that person a partner for life. Scripture says: *He who finds a wife finds a good thing.* Remember, God saw that Adam needed a human friend and mate. Human companionship is good and has its benefits. But it cannot take the place in your life that belongs only to God.

Neither are the actions of another human the answer to our dissatisfaction. Sometimes women say things like, if my husband would only talk to me more…or, if he would get home from work earlier…, I would be satisfied. And I have heard men say that if their wife would just lose weight or keep the house cleaner, they would be content in their marriage. Although they may enjoy these changes, they will not remove the emptiness that is existing in their soul.

Only God can bring genuine satisfaction. God is the One who created that empty space and only He can fill it. When your longing for God is filled, then you will be able to truly enjoy the people and things God has put in your life. What is really important, becomes important and what is not, you have the grace to ignore. You can then experience real satisfaction. The companionship we receive from our spouses and others is a blessing to our lives, but it is not the source of blessing for our lives. We must go to God daily to be filled with His presence to prevent ourselves from expecting to receive more from someone else than they are able to give.

We are much less frustrated when we accept people the way God has made them and accept wherever they are in their walk with Him. In reality, they are out of our control. They are God's business, not ours. Psalm 138 declares: *The LORD will perfect that which concerns me.* According to *The Spirit-Filled Life Bible*, the word perfect, **gamar**, refers to the completing, finishing, and perfecting of God's work in one's life.[17] God begins to work out His purposes in all of His children and He does not stop until it is absolutely and completely complete.

Meanwhile we must have grace for one another, just as God has shown grace toward us. Again, we can decide to look for the good and lovely in every person and situation as we look for the "if" found in Philippians 4:8 and apply it to our thoughts, *...if there is any virtue and if there is anything praiseworthy – meditate on these things.* Sometimes it is difficult to find something praiseworthy to think on concerning someone, in which case I try not to think much about them at all.

Leviticus 19:18 commands: *Do not seek revenge or bear a grudge against anyone among your people, but love your neighbor as yourself. I am the LORD.* In Matthew 18:23-35, Jesus shares a story that informs us that the person who holds a grudge will live in a prison (without bars) with tormentors. Those tormentors are things such as sleeplessness, depression, anxiety, anger and bitterness. We cannot deny the importance God puts on love and forgiveness, as He has demonstrated to us through the life of Jesus Christ and in repeated commands to love one another. He has even commanded us to love our enemies. After all, didn't He show His love toward us in Christ while we were still at enmity with Him? How do we love? We do it by the grace of God. Remember, love is not a *feeling* but a *choice* we make to *obey* God. He will enable us if we will make the decision and turn to Him for help. It is necessary if we are to live satisfied.

Moments at the Fountain

Reflection & Application

Things to Remember

- Satisfaction is a result of allowing God, not people, to be the one to fill the void in our life.

- Satisfaction is learned when God enables us to walk as a bondservant in love, grace and service toward others, putting their needs above our own.

- Forgiving yourself and others is necessary in order to live a satisfied and abundant life in Christ.

- God deals with us according to grace, even though it is undeserved. We should, therefore, deal with one another as God has dealt with us.

Philippians 2:5-8

> *Your attitude should be the same as that of Christ Jesus: Who, being in very nature God, did not consider equality with God something to be grasped, but made himself nothing, taking the very nature of a servant, being made in human likeness. And being found in appearance as a man, he humbled himself and became obedient to death—even death on a cross!*

Mark 11:25

Whenever you stand praying, forgive, if you have anything against anyone, so that your Father who is in heaven will also forgive you your transgressions.

Romans 13:8 (NLT)

Owe nothing to anyone—except for your obligation to love one another. If you love your neighbor, you will fulfill the requirements of God's law.

1 Corinthians 13:3-7 (NLT)

If I gave everything I have to the poor and even sacrificed my body, I could boast about it but if I didn't love others, I would have gained nothing. Love is patient and kind. Love is not jealous or boastful or proud or rude. It does not demand its own way. It is not irritable, and it keeps no record of being wronged. It does not rejoice about injustice but rejoices whenever the truth wins out. Love never gives up, never loses faith, is always hopeful, and endures through every circumstance.

Reflect & Grow

1. Think of a time you have put your expectations on someone else. How did it turn out? What are some of the ways that you put your expectations on your husband? Your children? Your friends? How might this result negatively?

2. How can you live as a bondservant to Christ? What do you need to change in your attitude in order to serve others?

3. How does having a servant's heart reduce striving with others?

4. Sanctification is a process in which we are to cooperate with God. What can you do, if anything, to help in this process?

5. What does Matthew 18:23-35 say about unforgiveness? Who is worthy to be the judge? What are the torturers that are unleashed on us when we refuse to forgive? Is there any one in your life that you need to release to God to free your heart of unforgiveness?

6. How can we keep our way pure? Read Psalm 119:9-24. How might it help us to maintain satisfaction in the midst of our interacting with difficult people by asking God to open our eyes to others around us?

7. Think of some situations where you could have taken up the Philippians 4:8 approach. Is it possible that it would have changed the results of the situation? How?

8. Think of a time when you allowed someone else's opinion of you affect how you viewed yourself. If this same situation happened today, would you feel differently? What could you do to begin identifying yourself as the person whom God has declared you are?

9. How might you serve sacrificially, putting others' needs before your own? Think of something kind to do towards someone today.

10. Read Romans 12:10-18 and make a list of the ways Paul encourages us to interact with others.

Prayer

Thank You, Lord, for Your amazing love and grace. Help me to give Your love and grace to others as You have given it to me. Thank You for the satisfaction and joy that results from loving You and Your household. In Jesus' name, I pray.

Confession

I am filled with the love of God and freely show forth His love to others. I have been forgiven my debt to God; therefore, with His help, I graciously extend forgiveness to those who hurt me, praying for them and releasing them to God's care.

Chapter 9 ———————————————

Adjusting Your Focus

———————————————————

Then he said to them, "Watch out! Be on your
guard against all kinds of greed; a man's life does not
consist in the abundance of his possessions."
Luke 12:15

How many people do you know who are looking for satisfaction in things? Western society is materialistic, and material things are a popular substitute in the search for satisfaction. You won't have to think long to think of someone whose life is focused on increasing their possessions. This worldly value has even crept into the church. People allow things, and the debt accumulated to purchase them, to control their lives. Never mind the budget. Never mind the needs of the children. Never mind the bondage of debt that will keep them from doing the things God is calling them to do. We are excited with the initial purchase. Again, there is a sense of satisfaction; but, a week later, our enthusiasm has dwindled. A month later, we are experiencing the same symptoms of dissatisfaction we had before our new purchase. The bills roll in and our satisfaction disappears. Often, we contemplate the next purchase while complaining about not having any "free" money, as though that will bring us some satisfaction once again.

Think about it. What would happen to your sense of satisfaction if you were wiped out of material things? People can become so *focused* on things that a sudden loss can lead them to think they have nothing to live for any longer. This was seen in 1929 when the stock market crashed and many committed suicide. What thieves things can be!

In the Sermon on the Mount, Jesus warned people about laying up treasures on the earth; earthly treasures cannot make us feel safe. In Luke 12:15, we read: *Then he said to them, 'Watch out! Be on your guard against all kinds of greed; a man's life does not consist in the abundance of his possessions.'* Most people think possessions will bring them satisfaction, but in reality, they subtly rob us of the only satisfaction that really lasts. Why? It is because our human tendency is to pull away from God as the value of our possessions increases. The more possessions we have, the more we tend to rely on them for security rather than God. This is why Jesus said in Matthew 19:24: *Again I tell you, it is easier for a camel to go through the eye of a needle than for a rich man to enter the kingdom of God.* It is less likely for a wealthy man, who has an accumulation of things, to come to God. The rich man looks at his riches and fails to recognize his need for God. It is not wrong to have riches, but the truth is money and the things money purchases can easily become competition for the time and devotion God desires for Himself alone.

If God has blessed you with wealth, guard yourself from looking to those riches as your provision for life, happiness and contentment. It is a good idea to offer back a minimum of one tenth of your increase to your local fellowship where you are fed the Word of God. This discipline helps you to keep your priorities in the right order. Those who become lovers of things have a difficult time following this principle, and they usually try to justify not doing so. This is a sure sign they are trying to serve both mammon and God, of which the Bible is clear you cannot do. Therefore, I have to ask, "Can one really afford NOT to tithe?" The Old Testament teaches the tithe is accursed (Joshua 6-7) and if not given for God's use, will be lost any way through one or many different forms, i.e. doctor bills, repair bills, etc. Why not give back to God for the advancement of His Kingdom instead? Although there are differences of opinion concerning whether the tithe is commanded for the church today or if it was one of the many ordinances that existed for those of Old Testament times, one's giving or lack of reveals where one's focus is – on one's selfish self and temporary worldly pleasures or on God and His eternal Kingdom. The Apostle Paul in a letter to the Corinthians addressed giving: *Let each one do just as he has purposed in his heart; not grudgingly or under compulsion; for God loves a cheerful giver* (2 Corinthians 9: 7). Then in verse 8, he reveals the source from which a heart to give comes: *And God is able to make all grace abound to you, that always having all sufficiency in everything, you may have an abundance for every good deed.* This verse alone impacts me to give. How about you?

Even though His emphasis was on not neglecting the weightier things of the law, we can conclude from Matthew 23:23 that Jesus thought the tithe should not be neglected.Speaking to the religious leaders of the day, He says: *Woe to you, teachers of the law and Pharisees, you hypocrites! You give a tenth of your spices—mint, dill and cumin. But you have neglected the more important matters of the law—justice, mercy and faithfulness. You should have practiced the latter,* **without neglecting the former** (Emphasis mine).

Material things are not evil in themselves, but they do rob us of our satisfaction when they have become our first love. Look at how the obsessive desire for more things has provoked innumerable get rich quick schemes and gambling opportunities. The prophet Jeremiah describes such foolishness in Jeremiah 17:11, *Like a partridge that hatches eggs it did not lay is the man who gains riches by unjust means. When his life is half gone, they will desert him, and in the end he will prove to be a fool.*

I have seen families destroyed because women fell for the deception that to be "somebody," they needed to go into the job market and become successful in a profession. Some think they need a career to give their children all the things they desire, but the presence of their mother's love and guidance is what they really need. All the purchased things are substitutes for the relationship with mom. I am not condemning the women who work outside of the home. I have done the same. I am simply saying to do so in order to provide our children with many "things" may actually do them more harm than good.

Material things are temporary and do not build the character of our children. Giving our children everything they desire prepares them to live out their lives searching for satisfaction in *temporary* things. We need to accept that things are not going to fulfill them, just as they haven't fulfilled us. Our children need a relationship with Christ, just as we do. Yet, how many of us have acknowledged that truth in our minds, but we have not attempted to change our lifestyle or redirect our drive to acquire more and more. Be sure to pray and ask for God's guidance in making decisions concerning your profession, your children and balancing your home life. He will be faithful to order your steps to accomplish His purpose in the lives of your family members when you seek His will and wisdom. For some, it works for both parents to work outside the home; and for others, it is not what God's wisdom directs.

We must serve God with our whole heart. We cannot serve God whole-heartedly and have acquiring riches as our goal at the same time. Being double-minded, looking at the world's riches and at the same time attempting to follow Jesus, results in dissatisfaction. Remember what Jesus said in Matthew 6:24: *No one can serve two masters. Either he will hate the one and love the other, or he will be devoted to the one and despise the other.* Be single minded. You cannot serve both God and money. In the book of James we are told not to be double-minded, meaning not to be undecided or vacillating. James tells us that the double-minded person is unstable in all his ways and should not expect to receive from God.

For some, acquiring an education has become their first love. Education is good and can be used by God for the fulfillment of His purpose and plan for your life. However, if you allow a degree to replace God as your primary focus, then higher education can be a thing that robs you of satisfaction.

A warning for parents: Without a solid foundation in the Word of God, I am afraid that much higher education destroys our kids instead of helping them to fulfill the purpose God desires for them. The statistics are staggering concerning the number of high school students who attend church before entering college, then end up turning away from their belief in God. There are many professors in our schools and colleges who teach very convincingly against the reality of God; therefore, we need to be sure to build a solid biblical foundation in the lives of our children before they go to college, and help them prayerfully select the schools they will attend.

There is nothing wrong with things in themselves. There is nothing wrong with education, recognition or position. It is the danger of allowing them to become your *focus* or goal for life that is the problem. Take a look at the Apostle Paul. Although he was highly educated and had many advantages in life, making Jesus Christ the goal of his life is what brought him satisfaction. It wasn't his money, education, recognition, or profession that satisfied him. It was Jesus. He had concluded that there was nothing else in this world that could compare to Christ. Philippians 3:10-15: *I want to know Christ and the power of his resurrection and the fellowship of sharing in his sufferings, becoming like him in his death, and so, somehow, to attain to the resurrection from the dead. Not that I have already obtained all this, or have already been made perfect, but I press on to take hold of that for which Christ Jesus took hold of me. Brothers, I do not consider myself yet to have taken hold of it. But one thing I do: Forgetting what is behind and straining toward what is ahead, I press on toward the goal to win the prize for which God has called me heavenward in Christ Jesus. All of us who are mature should take such a view of things. And if on some point you think differently, that too God will make clear to you.* Paul says he leaves the past behind. He has his mind focused on his goal of becoming like Christ.

A number of years ago, I had prospered as a small business owner. My previous husband had abandoned me with two children and I was faced with a financial dilemma. God gave me the idea and knowledge to begin a communications company in order to provide for my children and myself.

But, as the company grew, my whole identity became wrapped up in being a successful business woman. Eventually I met my husband of today and he came to work with me. We made a great team and the business grew even more, until we had three business locations. I always thought of the business as belonging to me, however, because I began it from scratch and did all the ground work to get the business off the ground. Getting those first customers was difficult and it took a lot of perseverance not to quit.

One day God spoke to us to begin to prepare for ministry. We were already taking classes and spending what time we could at the church we attended. We were so hungry for Jesus, but the business required a lot of our time and energy. It was definitely a huge part of my life. I was about to find out what meant more to me – my relationship with God or the business.

One morning, I heard God's "still small voice" within tell me to sell the business. I loved God, but to sell the business was asking a lot. I had gone from barely surviving to finally enjoying the fruit of my labor. Would God really require me to sacrifice the business and walk away from it? I was very much aware that God desired for me to find my identity in Him. I realized it had become wrapped up in being that successful business woman. To sell the business was to lose the identity I had grown comfortable in!

You see, things consist of more than material objects. Things can be position, recognition, achievements, organizations, societies, and education. Although I knew God was the source and reason for my success, somehow the business had taken a place in my heart that should only belong to Him! In order to truly benefit from life's available joys, it is key that we guard our hearts and deny anything, aside from God, from becoming our primary focus in life and, thereby, robbing us of our energy for God, His kingdom and righteousness.

Of course, there were many things I felt I had to consider before selling the business – like my husband, son, daughter and her husband, and my brother, who were all employed by the business, in addition to another husband-wife team and two other singles. I concluded if it were God telling me to sell, there was nothing left to consider. I stepped out in faith and obedience to God and put the business up for sale. God left me no room to change my mind. The entire business sold the first day listed on the market! Thirty days later we were asking, "What next God?"

Although there have been challenges and even times when I could not see His hand, I have never regretted my obedience to Him in removing this business from interfering with my relationship with God and serving Him as a minister of the Gospel. Growing in relationship with God and learning to walk by faith in Him is how I want to continue my journey on earth. A growing, intimate relationship with our Father and Lord Jesus is the only thing any of us really need. It is the one thing that really counts!

To be satisfied we need to keep our eyes on Jesus. We should surrender our hearts to Him and dedicate ourselves to doing all we can to become more like Him each day. This is accomplished by allocating our time and resources according to how they will help achieve our goal, which, as Christians, should be to become like Christ.

Jesus once said to Peter in Matthew 16:23: *Get behind Me, Satan! You are a stumbling block to Me; for you are not setting your mind on God's interests, but man's.* There is a danger of becoming stumbling blocks to ourselves when we set our minds on worldly things instead of God and His righteousness. I have determined to adjust and readjust, as necessary, my focus on Christ. How about you?

Moments at the Fountain

Reflection & Application

Things to Remember

- An individual truly focused on Christ and their growth in Him will experience satisfaction.

- An item's value is determined by the price someone is willing to pay for it. The value of Christ's life determined the value of yours, if you belong to Christ.

- Giving children everything they desire prepares them to live out their lives searching for satisfaction in temporary things instead of in a relationship with God.

- The key is to guard your heart from allowing anything to take or share God's place in what defines your life – giving you your identity.

Romans 12:2

Do not conform any longer to the pattern of this world, but be transformed by the renewing of your mind. Then you will be able to test and approve what God's will is—his good, pleasing and perfect will.

Luke 12:15

...Be on your guard against all kinds of greed; a man's life does not consist in the abundance of his possessions.

Jeremiah 17:11

Like a partridge that hatches eggs it did not lay is the man who gains riches by unjust means. When his life is half gone, they will desert him, and in the end he will prove to be a fool.

Colossians 3:1

Since, then, you have been raised with Christ, set your hearts on things above, where Christ is, seated at the right hand of God.

Reflect & Grow

1. When do things rob us of satisfaction?

2. What things are keeping you from Christ, robbing you of true satisfaction? What steps can you take to change this?

3. What happens when you try to serve two masters? Matthew 6:24.

4. What is the view Paul shares in Philippians 3:13-16 that mature believers should have?

5. What is a cluttered heart? According to 1 Chronicles 29:19, why should we desire an uncluttered heart? Is your heart cluttered?

6. Where should our focus be according to Philippians 3:17-21? How can we maintain that focus according to 1 Timothy 4:13?

7. What has been defining your life (i.e. I shared about a season when being a successful business owner defined my life)? What should define your life? Why? What is the truth concerning what gives your life genuine value? What steps can you take to begin to realign your thinking with this truth?

8. What is meant by the term double-minded? Read James 1:6-8. How does this prevent you from experiencing satisfaction?

9. Jesus tells us to do as He does (John 13:15) and Paul tells us to do as he does as far as he follows Christ. What do we need to do in order to do this? Read Proverbs 4:21.

10. What is it that brought Paul satisfaction? Read Philippians 3:10-15.

Prayer

Father, I thank You to order my steps in Your Word. Help me to allocate my time and resources in such a way to advance my goal to become more like Christ and thereby glorify You in all that I say, think and do.

Confession

I am focused on becoming like Christ and I purpose to love and serve Him with my whole heart, mind, soul and strength. I allocate my time and resources for this goal.

Chapter 10 ————————————————

Accepting God's Rule

Know, recognize, and understand therefore this day and
turn your mind and heart to it that the Lord is God in the
heavens above and upon the earth beneath; there is no other.
Deuteronomy 4:39 (NIV)

*I*n order to experience genuine satisfaction, it is imperative you come to know God. Of course, God is so awesome you can never know Him fully, but you can continuously pursue Him and increasingly grow in an intimate knowledge of His Person. As you seek Him, He will reveal Himself to you so that you know you can trust Him. This pursuit is the only way to develop confidence in God. Without confidence in God – His character, love and ways, it is impossible to truly experience fulfillment and satisfaction in life. Unless you trust God, you will not be able to accept the things in life that you do not understand. It is only as you know God that you can have peace and confidence no matter who you are, what you have done, where you find yourself today, and no matter what circumstance surrounds you.

There are things you can do to increase your knowledge of God and your trust in Him. Daily time spent in prayer, for example, is essential for knowing God. As you pray, don't forget to be still and allow Him to talk to you. So many times we are so busy talking He cannot get a word in edge-wise. As you spend time with Him, your knowledge and relationship with Him will deepen.

It is also important to spend time in the Bible because God has revealed, therein, all we need to know about Himself and His ways. The Scripture says that He has given us in the Bible everything that pertains to life and godliness. We can know how God will respond in various types of situations because He is the same yesterday, today and forever. You will discover that He is not only unchanging, but always faithful to His Word and character. What peace this revelation brings to our souls.

Obedience to God is equally important to our spiritual knowledge and growth. As you grow in your obedience to God, you will discover that your knowledge about Him increases as well. Yes, God rewards our obedience by sharing His secrets and unveiling more of Himself to us. Psalm 25:14: *The secret of the LORD is for those who fear Him and He will make them know His covenant.*

Studying the names of God is another great way to grow in your relationship and knowledge of God. God reveals His character through the names He gives to Himself. Just as we know more about a woman when she is called mother or wife, or more about a man who is called husband or father, we know more about God by His names. There are several good books on the names of God. One I have used in my studies is: *My Father's Names* by Elmer L. Towns. The following paragraph is from that book.

"He is Jehovah Roi, the One who cares for all the needs of His sheep. He is El Shaddai, the God who supplies all my needs. He is El Elyon, the Possessor of Heaven and earth. He is great to the superlative degree. He is El Olam, the Everlasting God available to His people throughout the ages, yet remains a mystery and a secret to mere human minds. He is El Gibbor. In battle He is a divine Warrior and in uncertain times He is a divine Rock. God always supports His children with His strength unless they insist on trusting on their own strength. He is Jehovah Melek a benevolent King who establishes laws for the good of His subjects and He deserves our total obedience. As Jehovah Sabaoth, He is the Commander of the angels. He sends these angels to guard and protect us from harm and as we follow Him into battle, we know the outcome is certain to be Victorious! As our divine Master, Adonai, we can expect Him to supply us with all the resources and provision we need in order to live out every situation He allows us to be in; and to carry out all that He calls us to do. God is Elohim, the God who is the source of all there is. He is life, person, spirit, self-existent, One, unchangeable and unlimited. And as the plural Elohim implies, God is three-in-one, the Trinity. God is the self-existent God who is the eternal source of life—He who will be who He will be, whose existence depends on no other. God also desires to be known to His children by the intimate name of Pater as our loving Father. Through Christ we are invited not to cower before Him in fear but to enter into an intimate family relationship with Him."[18]

Growing in an understanding that God is sovereign, omnipotent (all-powerful), omniscient (all-knowing), omnipresent (simultaneously everywhere present), and immutable (unchanging), and grasping the greatness of His love has proven to be crucial in building my confidence in God and accepting His hand on my life. Understanding and believing *by faith* that God is who He says He is brings you to this point of acceptance. You begin to accept His governing of your life, and the circumstances you find yourself in during various seasons. You accept those things you do not understand, and the things you cannot change.

If we are to be satisfied in this life, although God's love is unfathomable, we must have some knowledge of its greatness toward us. God is Love. *And so we know and rely on the love God has for us. Whoever lives in love lives in God, and God in him* (I John 4:16). Because God is Love, He is forever giving of Himself to others to bring blessings to them. Love is not a garment He wears that can be taken off. The Bible tells us He Himself is Love. He cannot divest Himself of it. Therefore, everything God does and allows comes forth from His love.

Have you ever known anyone who would die for their enemy? God the Son left heaven and came to earth as a man. He was brutally beaten, rejected, scorned and crucified because He desired to reconcile you to Himself. He did this when you were at enmity with Him. Now that is love beyond our comprehension! This is a love that never fails and never fades! A love you can count on! Who has or ever will demonstrate their love toward you as He has done? Romans 5:8 says: *But God demonstrates his own love for us in this: While we were still sinners, Christ died for us.* How do we accept His love into our lives? It is necessary to accept His love by faith.

God is supreme in power, rank, authority and work. There is no one and nothing like God. He is supreme over all the earth and everything in it. There is no greater power or authority. Everything that exists was created by Him for His purposes. He is all-powerful and in control of every situation (Isaiah 45:5-7).

When I say God is sovereign, I am saying nothing happens in the heavens and earth without God's permission. Our God rules! God made this point to King Nebuchadnezzar in the Book of Daniel. Although warned to the contrary, Nebuchadnezzar claimed credit for himself for the greatness of his empire. God gave him a dream. Daniel, interpreting King Nebuchadnezzar's dream, says: *Seven times will pass by for you until you acknowledge that the Most High is sovereign over the kingdoms of men and gives them to anyone he wishes. The command to leave the stump of the tree with its roots means that your kingdom will be restored to you when you acknowledge that Heaven rules* (Daniel 4:25b-26). *Immediately what had been said about Nebuchadnezzar was fulfilled. He was driven away from people and ate grass like cattle...* (Daniel 4:33). The story continues with Nebuchadnezzar stating in Daniel 4:34-35, *At the end of that time, I, Nebuchadnezzar, raised my eyes toward heaven, and my sanity was restored. Then I praised the Most High; I honored and glorified him who lives forever. His dominion is an eternal dominion; his kingdom endures from generation to generation. All the peoples of the earth are regarded as nothing. He does as he pleases with the powers of heaven and the peoples of the earth. No one can hold back his hand or say to him: "What have you done?"*

Realizing God's sovereign rule is intertwined with His love, in all He does and allows in our lives, gives us confidence. We know that everything God allows to happen is only allowed by Him because He will use it for good according to His sovereign, eternal purpose and plan for our lives.

Does this mean we will understand it? I can tell you we will not understand everything God does or allows in our lives. Just as little children cannot understand the decisions adults make for them, we are children in comparison to God and unable to understand all the whys of the way He rules over our lives. Isaiah 55:8-9 puts it well, declaring that God's thoughts and ways are higher than ours. Many times we want to ask, how can any good come out of this circumstance? But when we know God, we know His character requires Him to turn everything to good to accomplish His purposes (Romans 8:28). Knowing this, we can accept by faith His plan for our lives and we can be satisfied in it.

Although God is sovereign, man still has free will and is accountable to God for His choices. However, God's plans are so sovereign and He is so powerful that He can intervene in our choices and circumstances to perfect His plan. In other words, God rules and He also overrules, and no man, angel, demon or circumstance of life can stop His plan from coming to pass. Although God has given me free will, there are times when He intervenes and overrules my choice. Praise the Lord! At other times, however, He allows me to make wrong choices. But when He allows this, He has a plan and purpose to use it for my good in bringing me closer to Him and molding me into His image. However, we still experience consequences of our choices and if choices are deliberate rebellion, we can expect to be disciplined. This is because God's very essence is love and He rules supremely over all! Even in the area of correction and discipline, Hebrews 12:10 tells us the Father's discipline is a manifestation of His love for His children: *Our fathers disciplined us for a little while as they thought best; but God disciplines us for our good, that we may share in his holiness.*

One of God's moral attributes is goodness. God is the only and final standard for goodness. Therefore, everything He does is worthy of approval. In Luke 18:19, Jesus declares, *No one is good — except God alone.* We can rest in the love and goodness of God! What confidence this gives us in living out the circumstances of our lives. And it is this confidence in God that enables us to live satisfied.

Several years ago I was at the beach with a group of women for a ladies' retreat. One morning my friend and I stood to wait for the elevator to reach our floor. Just as we stepped onto the elevator, there was suddenly a huge group of senior citizens rushing to join us. They quickly squeezed into the small elevator forcing me against the back wall. As they pushed their way on, I yelled, "No! Stop!" I knew without a doubt the elevator could not safely hold so many people. Just as I cried out, the doors closed with the last few people pressed against the door. Needless to say, with all the bodies packed in the elevator like sardines, it was hot. I looked up to the ceiling and there was no fan in the elevator. The elevator was descending, and when I saw our floor number appear, the elevator did not stop. The elevator continued downward until it stopped between floors. We were overloaded! And, we were stuck!

Right then and there I had to choose whether to panic or trust God. It was one of those opportunities when the reality of your faith is proven or not proven. My friend was pressed against the elevator phone. She squeezed it out of its cradle and called the emergency number. There was no answer! She called again. Again, no answer.

The air thinned quickly, and perspiration was dripping off of our faces. I began to talk to God. I said, "I know you are sovereign and all-powerful. I know you can get us out of this elevator, if You want to. Father, if it is not our time to come meet You face to face, then I am asking You to save us. If it is Your will for us to come to You, then Your will be done." I had a vision of an image of bright, yet comforting, light as I was talking to God, and it was as though I was out of my body. I was at perfect peace knowing my God was in control of all things and nothing could accidentally take my life. God would have to allow it.

While experiencing this vision, God talked to me concerning some difficult things that were going on in my life. I had just been betrayed by my best friend. I was feeling rejected and hurt. At this point in my Christian maturity, I wondered if there was something wrong with me spiritually that would bring this negative treatment towards me. God impressed upon me His love. He let me know my thoughts were untrue. He told me I was His workmanship and He was well pleased with me. He convinced me I was valuable to Him. He shared with me that He had plans for me to include some kingdom assignments. It was not time for me to go to Him yet.

As our conversation ended people began to panic. My friend began to sing a song to the Lord, and we all joined in, even though the air was thinning and we knew we were using more air by doing so. We continued to try the phone and finally someone answered. Soon, the doors were pried open – Praise the Lord! God touched me that day and infused a sense of significance into my very soul. I felt He had stopped the elevator just to speak to me, even though I know He may have spoken to others, who were on that elevator, at the very same time He spoke to me. It could be that the enemy of our souls had planned to hurt all of us on that elevator, and God allowed him to go this far but no further, just to get me into a place where He could talk to me and I could listen. My God rules; and my life is held in His hands and His hands alone! If you are a Christian, the same holds true for you!

Our heavenly Father is omnipresent. God is everywhere simultaneously. There is not a place where God is not. Psalm 139:5 says about God: *You both precede and follow me. You place your hand of blessing on my head.* Realizing God is with you, wherever you are, is a great comfort, because God's omnipresence ensures His power. Since He is always with His children, He is able to work in their lives at all times. He is there when you are lonely, when you are afraid, when you are weak, and when you are in danger. He brings you His love, comfort, strength, wisdom and power. He guides you when you don't know where to go. He will always be right there, wherever you are, and ready to meet whatever need you may have. God confirms this in Hebrews 13:5: *Never will I leave you; never will I forsake you.*

Another wonderful truth is God is immutable—unchanging! He will never be more than what He is right now and what He has always been, and He will never be less. He is all in all. God spoke to Malachi, as written in Malachi 3:6: *I the Lord do not change.* Change happens to us without our consent. Our circumstances change and the people in our lives change. Our experiences in life sometimes mold and change us. But we can be satisfied and at peace knowing our God never changes!

God is all-powerful (omnipotent). He doesn't derive power from another source but He is the source of His Own power. For he spoke, and it came to be; he commanded, and it stood firm (Psalm 33:9). There is nothing more powerful than God.

Your throne was established long ago;
*   you are from all eternity.*
The seas have lifted up, O LORD,
*   the seas have lifted up their voice;*
*   the seas have lifted up their pounding waves.*
Mightier than the thunder of the great waters,
*   mightier than the breakers of the sea—*
*   the LORD on high is mighty (Psalm 93:2-4)*

As a child of God, you are able to draw on the power of your Father. *I can do everything through him who gives me strength*, (Philippians 4:13). It is the unlimited strength of our all-powerful God that works everything for good to those He has called (Romans 8:28). Also, 2 Corinthians 9:8: *And God is able to make all grace abound to you, so that in all things at all times, having all that you need, you will abound in every good work.*

Our God is also omniscient or all knowing. Wayne Grudem in his book, *Bible Doctrine*, defines God's knowledge, saying: "God fully knows Himself and all things actual and possible in one simple and eternal act."[19]

God's knowledge never changes or grows. He has always been and will always be omniscient. God has known all things from all eternity— that which would happen and that which He would do. God knows everything! He knows everything about you and He is totally aware of His creation. He knows your thoughts and desires. Psalm 139:1-18 confirms this message:

O LORD, you have searched me
*   and you know me.*
You know when I sit and when I rise;
*   you perceive my thoughts from afar.*
You discern my going out and my lying down;
*   you are familiar with all my ways.*
Before a word is on my tongue
*   you know it completely, O LORD.*
You hem me in—behind and before;
*   you have laid your hand upon me.*

Such knowledge is too wonderful for me,
    too lofty for me to attain.
Where can I go from your Spirit?
Where can I flee from your presence?
If I go up to the heavens, you are there;
    if I make my bed in the depths, you are there.
If I rise on the wings of the dawn,
    if I settle on the far side of the sea,
Even there your hand will guide me;
    your right hand will hold me fast.
If I say, "Surely the darkness will hide me
    and the light become night around me,"
Even the darkness will not be dark to you;
    the night will shine like the day,
    for darkness is as light to you.
For you created my inmost being;
    you knit me together in my mother's womb.
I praise you because I am fearfully and wonderfully made;
    your works are wonderful, I know that full well.
My frame was not hidden from you
    when I was made in the secret place.
When I was woven together in the depths of the earth,
    your eyes saw my unformed body.
All the days ordained for me
    were written in your book
    before one of them came to be.
How precious to me are your thoughts, O God!
How vast is the sum of them!
Were I to count them,
    they would outnumber the grains of sand.
When I awake,
I am still with you.

As a Christian develops a deeper understanding of God, by experiencing Him through life's circumstances and studying His attributes and character as revealed in Scripture, confidence in God deepens. Understanding God loves you, is always with you, is all-powerful, all-knowing, unchanging, and that His rule is sovereign over all heaven and earth, gives you every reason to be satisfied. You realize you are in the best hands—the hands of God!

Moments at the Fountain

Reflection & Application

Things to Remember

- A good recipe for satisfaction is to grow in confidence of who God is. Accept who He is. Trust His hand on your life and continually seek to grow in relationship with Him.

- We can be satisfied and at peace knowing our God is immutable; knowing He is omnipresent, omniscient and omnipotent; knowing His goodness and receiving His love.

- We accept God's love, receiving it into our hearts, by an act of faith.

Deuteronomy 4:39 (NIV)
Know, recognize, and understand therefore this day and turn your mind and heart to it that the Lord is God in the heavens above and upon the earth beneath; there is no other.

1 Samuel 12:22
For the Lord will not abandon His people on account of His great name, because the Lord has been pleased to make you a people for Himself.

Psalm 33:14,15
From His dwelling place He looks out on all the inhabitants of the earth, He who fashions the hearts of them all, He who understands all their works.

Psalm 100:3

Know that the Lord Himself is God; it is He who has made us, and not we ourselves; we are His people and the sheep of His pasture.

Psalm 100:19

The Lord has established His throne in the heavens; and His sovereignty rules over all.

Psalm 75:7

But God is the Judge; He puts down one, and exalts another.

Reflect & Grow

1. Share a challenging time in your life which you found difficult to accept, yet later you realized the hand of God was in it after all.

2. Are there any situations in your present life that you are struggling with? If you are comfortable sharing, do so and explore how you might find peace and satisfaction in the midst of it.

3. Why do you think we struggle with accepting God in our difficult times? What adjustment in our thinking do we need to make in order to be at peace with this?

4. Does it bring you peace to know that all things in heaven and earth are being governed by a loving God who rules, and overrules, according to the counsel of His will? Why or why not?

5. Does it comfort you to know that God will fulfill His purpose and plan in your life? Why?

6. Describe the difference in a life that has heard of God's love and the one who has received His love. How does your life show that you have received His love for you?

7. Describe God's character as you know it.

8. Look at the names God has revealed Himself as listed in this chapter. Think about and share a time you experienced God as who His names reveal.

9. Without confidence in God's character, what will you do in trying circumstances?

10. Think about and describe the characteristics of God listed below. Then think about what this means to you personally.

God's love -

God's goodness-

God's sovereignty-

God's immutability-

God's omniscience-

God's omnipotence-

God's omnipresence-

Prayer

Father, You are the Lord of my life, my king and sovereign God. As awesome as I know You are, I know You are so much more. Help me, Lord, to increase in a knowledge of You. Help me to walk in obedience and to trust Your rule in my life regardless what I see in the circumstances surrounding me. Thank You for anything good or great that is accomplished through my life. Help me remember that it is You who exalts and brings low. To You be all the glory in everything! In Jesus' name, I pray.

Confession

God rules over all the heaven and earth. He is my all in all, the Source of everything I need for any and all situations. He is my tower of refuge and strength; and because He reigns victorious, so do I.

Chapter 11

Defining Your Life

But you are the ones chosen by God, chosen for the
high calling of priestly work, chosen to be a holy people,
God's instruments to do his work and speak out for him, to tell
others of the night-and-day difference he made for you.
1 Peter 2:9 (MSG)

*I*n the previous chapter we established that genuine satisfaction is not available without accepting who God is and that His rule is over all. Another area of acceptance we need to address is accepting yourself. Since the fall of man, men and women have struggled in the area of self-acceptance. Striving for self-worth and self-esteem continues to be an issue within the church, as well as outside of it. In order to live a satisfied life, however, you must learn to accept yourself as a new creation in Christ.

As 1 Peter 2:9 states, God chose *you*. He picked you out even before you were formed in your mother's womb, and He did so knowing every single detail of what your future would hold. *For you created my inmost being; you knit me together in my mother's womb* (Psalm 139:13). This holy, sovereign, all-powerful, all-knowing God Who is Creator of all that exists, chose you to become His adopted child and ambassador on earth. He knew your every thought and action, both good and evil, even before you experienced them yourself, and He chose you anyway!

The fact that God chose you makes you significant! God says you are righteous. You can accept you are righteous simply because He says so. You do not have to understand it; you only have to accept it. The Christian walk is a walk of faith. By faith you must accept you are a righteous child of God! You are not whom your father, mother or any other relative, friend or enemy has called you. Even if they say negative things about you, you are still the person God created you to be. You are not whom your boss or co-workers say you are. You are not whom your teachers said you are. You are whom God says you are and He says you are righteous! He says He has chosen you for a high calling. You are significant to God and He is the One who is all knowing. It is His opinion that counts. The Bible declares it with this question in Romans 8:31: *Who can be against you when God is for you?* No one else's opinion matters. Only the omniscient God, who has the power of life and death in His hands and is able to save your soul, really matters. He says He has chosen you to be holy and to be His instrument and voice on the earth.

We often hear people ask, "how much is that man worth?" – as if the worth of a man could be measured in dollars and cents. But think about this. We know the value of an item is determined by the price someone is willing to pay for it. Christ paid His life for you and me. The only life of infinite value was paid to purchase us from the hands of Satan. We then can conclude that we are of infinite value, even if we own nothing, because of the value of the blood of Jesus. His life is what was paid for us and gives us our worth. Why look for something less valuable than the Creator to find our identity? As Christians, our relationship and life in Christ should be what defines us.

Is there any person, or anything on this earth, that is greater, that has more power, that has more fame, that has more significance than the One who holds the stars and planets in the universe and sets the boundaries of the oceans? Is there anyone, or anything, that would carry a higher value than He who is the King of Kings and Lord of Lords, has always been and always will be? There is no one who even compares to Him. You must accept by faith whom God, your Creator, says you are if you are going to walk in genuine contentment and experience the abundant life Christ made available for all those who belong to Him.

True satisfaction comes as you realize God has made you valuable and has made you with a purpose. You are wonderfully complex and unique. There is no one else in the universe just like you. The way you look, feel, think – you may not understand yourself, but God does. It is not by accident you were born where you were, or that you have the interests you have. God was at work planning every area of your life even before you were born. He even formed the basic aspects of your personality while you were in your mother's womb. He designed you for the special purpose He has for you to fulfill on the earth. This unique purpose flows in conjunction with God's universal purpose for His people. That common purpose is to glorify God with all you think, say, and do, and through the joy of your relationship with Him. As you do this, His light will shine through you into a dark world and draw people to Christ.

Second Corinthians 3:5 tells us our competence comes from God. You have special abilities your sister or brother may not have. For example, one of my good friends is the most wonderful cook; while I am mediocre. Some are great in the garden and we call their thumbs green. Whereas, others, such as myself, only have green plants in the home if they are artificial. Some people I know are not so competent on the computer, while I can keyboard pretty well. Some have a gift of hospitality, others struggle to be hospitable. Some are quiet and some never meet a stranger. God gave specific abilities and personalities to each of us for His purposes.

God also gives spiritual gifts to those He chooses. First Peter 4:10 (NKJV) says: *As each one has received a gift, minister it to one another, as good stewards of the manifold grace of God.* God gives these gifts to bring purpose to our lives and glory to Him. He is gracious to allow us to partner with Him to advance His Kingdom on earth and encourage our brothers and sisters in Christ.

God is the architect of our lives, making us who we are. Education is a good thing. However, it is imperative to remember that a degree doesn't define you. Only God makes you who you are, not your degree or lack of one. He leads and guides; opens doors and experiences while closing others; gives natural and learned gifts and abilities; and, He sculpts our personalities and character. This same truth applies to those who attempt to define themselves by their awards, positions, and social status. In reality, although God may use the many tools and situations of life to form our lives, He is behind it all. God is who makes us all who we are. As long as that is understood, education can, indeed, be used by God to bring goodness into your life and the lives of others..

God allows experiences in your life—some good and some bad. But He uses all these experiences to mold character and personality. Romans 8:28 says: *And we know that in all things God works for the good of those who love him, who have been called according to his purpose.* God is always with you. Although He may not be the cause of everything that happens to you, He could intervene and stop anything from happening at any given moment. He does this at times and other times He does not. Therefore, we can say He does allow the things to happen that happen. He has control over everything. His promise to us is He will cause good to come out of our trials and circumstances as we trust Him in them. One such good is our transformation into the image of Christ (Romans 8:29). Our life experiences, and our responses to them, are used by God to shape us, to testify of God's goodness, faithfulness and power; and God equips us through our experiences so that we can help others who are hurting. Second Corinthians 1:4 says: *He comes alongside us when we go through hard times, and before you know it, he brings us alongside someone else who is going through hard times so that we can be there for that person just as God was there for us.*

So God is intimately involved in perfecting those He gave His life for, but the greatest proof of your value is that God left His lofty place in heaven to come to earth as a man and live as a man in order to die for you. You have worth because God gave His life, which has infinite value, for you. Who would pay such a high price for something of no value? You, my brothers and sisters, are more valuable than anything on the earth!

The following Scripture agrees with 1 Peter 2:9,

And they sang a new song:
Worthy! Take the scroll, open its seals.
Slain! Paying in blood, you bought men and women,
Bought them back from all over the earth, Bought them back for God.

Then you made them a Kingdom, Priests for our God,
Priest-Kings to rule over the earth (Revelation 5:9-10 MSG)

God declares you are a royal priesthood! Because you are a child of God, you have personal access to the throne room of heaven. Hebrews 4:16 says, *Let us then approach the throne of grace with confidence, so that we may receive mercy and find grace to help us in our time of need.*

The truth is, God didn't choose us because of anything we did or didn't do. He didn't choose us for any reason known to us. We only know that He chose to love us; and He desired to keep His promise to Abraham, whose descendants we are if we have faith in Jesus Christ. God spoke to Israel in Deuteronomy: *GOD wasn't attracted to you and didn't choose you because you were big and important—the fact is, there was almost nothing to you"*
He did it out of sheer love, keeping the promise he made to your ancestors (Deuteronomy 7:7-8 MSG).

As I talk about developing healthy self-esteem and recognizing your self-worth, I want to point out that I am not talking about having confidence in yourself without God. What I am talking about is having confidence in the person God makes you to be. In actuality, your confidence is in God. Paul in 2 Corinthians 12:9 (CEV) states it well: *...So if Christ keeps giving me his power, I will gladly brag about how weak I am. .* Acts 1:8 (NKJV) declares: *But you shall receive power when the Holy Spirit has come upon you; and you shall be witnesses to Me in Jerusalem, and in all Judea and Samaria, and to the end of the earth.*

Moses doubted his own strength and ability to carry out the work God called him to. You can read the full story in the book of Exodus. Moses began his ministry without confidence in himself. But he did have confidence in God. Because of God's grace and power, we are able to do the things He calls us to do. We must recognize and accept the limitations God has put on us. He has not given us the ability to do everything. But, at the same time, we should agree with God regarding who He says we are and concerning what He says He will do. We should have confidence that whatever God calls us to do He will also enable us to do. When we do not agree with God concerning His call on our lives, nor trust Him to enable us to be obedient to that call, God calls our disagreement *unbelief.* Unbelief is a sin. The effect of unbelief is seen throughout the history of the Church.

For example, many are caught up on the performance merry-go-round. They believe they must meet certain standards of performance in order to feel good about themselves. They tend to set standards for others as well. In both cases, they are setting themselves up for failure and disappointment.

On the other hand, you may be unusually talented and experience great success performing your way through life. If this is the case, I caution you not to mistake pride for positive self-worth. God insists we look to Him for our enablement. If you are looking to yourself for security and value, there will eventually be some failure or form of discipline intended to turn you toward Him. He insists to be first place in your life and He desires to partner with you in every endeavor. Remember God is your source for everything you need in life. He is your life!

This important truth is seen in Deuteronomy 8 in the warning Moses gives to the Israelites just before entering the promised land. They have seen and lived in God's supernatural provision while in the wilderness. The warning was concerning the possibility of the Israelites forgetting God's sovereign hand in his provision for them when given through the ordinary channels that were in their future, such as harvesting an abundance of crops. Moses warned the Israelites against saying: *My power and the strength of my hands have produced this wealth for me* (Deuteronomy 8:17). This viewpoint would, indeed, be heresy.

God's solution for our sin of arrogance, and every other behavioral problem, is wrapped up in what Christ did for us at Calvary. When I think about Christ hanging on the cross, I think about how God placed all my sins, both past and future, on Him. The Bible tells us the wrath of God was poured out on Him so that Jesus cried out, *Father, why have you forsaken me?* When Jesus finally said, *It is finished.* He was literally saying, our penalty was "paid in full." Words you might see at the bottom of a bill that no longer has a balance due.

So your sins were paid for in *full* thousands of years ago, long before you were even born. When you accept Christ as your Savior, you are accepting Christ's sacrifice on the cross as payment for every sin you would commit for your entire life. Your sins – past, present and future – have been paid for in full. This is not a license to sin, however. If someone takes it as that, they most likely have not had a true conversion experience. When the Spirit of God comes to dwell within, although you are still in process and may fail in your Christian walk at times, a desire to live for God is always present. A desire to live right is in the heart of all of God's children. Ezekiel prophesied of this changed heart – Ezekiel 11:19-20: *I will give them an undivided heart and put a new spirit in them; I will remove from them their heart of stone and give them a heart of flesh. Then they will follow my decrees and be careful to keep my laws. They will be my people, and I will be their God.*

I think many believe some sins are worse than others. Some sins, they believe, carry a heavier penalty. Some think they are going to heaven but do not believe God is pleased with them. Is that you? Do you think God's holiness is less grieved by some sins and more grieved by others? It is true, that as our Father, sins that have a greater effect on people cause Him more grief, i.e. adultery affects many people; murder can affect many people, etc. The Bible tells us, however, that as far as His holiness is concerned, to be guilty of one violation of the law is to be guilty of the whole law. He is grieved by all sin! No matter what the severity of our sin, however, the blood of Jesus washed away the penalty of all sin equally. Let's choose to agree with what the Bible says! Only in accepting the biblical truths, concerning the grace of God, found in Christ Jesus, can we experience real satisfaction.

Is it possible for a person to sin more than God will forgive? Can a person fill up or overflow God's capacity to forgive and redeem? If you are a child of God, the only way God would pour out His wrath on you is if He chose to ignore the wrath He poured out on Christ at Calvary. He would not dishonor Christ like that. He would not dismiss the value of what Christ did on the cross. *God made him who had no sin to be sin for us, so that in him we might become the righteousness of God* (2 Corinthians 5:21). When you accepted Jesus' gift, God imputed the righteousness that belonged to Christ to you. It is yours. You cannot do anything to become any less righteous, or any more righteous, because your righteousness is *His* righteousness! Just as Adam's sin was imputed to those born of Him, Jesus' righteousness was imputed to those born of Christ.

Sin affects us and is destructive. There are times when God has to discipline us just as we do our children. But it is key to understand that when we act sinfully, we are acting below what God has called and enabled us to do. Robert McGee, author of *In Search of Significance* draws the picture of a man suddenly losing his mind and thinking he is a dog. The man gets down on all fours and begins barking. The question he asked: Does this make the man a dog? Of course not; he is still a man despite what he thinks about himself or acts like![20]

For those who are born again in Christ, sometimes we act like that man who thought he was a dog, except that we think we are worthless and inept. We don't realize we are recreated by the hand of God. We underestimate our value. Does our wrongful thinking change the fact that God values us greatly? No. We have great value in God's eyes no matter what we think, but we don't experience much of the good consequence of belonging to God when we are stuck in unbelief. Author McGee explains that understanding the difference between our *actions* and our *value* enables us to reject our performance without devaluing ourselves. McGee goes on to say that unless we break free of this kind of wrongful thinking, we will never know who we truly are.[21]

I fully agree. If you do not know who you are, then you will never be able to mature in Christ. How many Christians have been walking with the Lord for their entire life, but have made little progress in Christ-like thinking or behavior? Very often, a lack of understanding about the total effectiveness of the cross of Jesus is at the root of their powerlessness to lead successful Christian lives. To become a genuinely satisfied Christian, who walks into the fullness of your destiny, you must agree with God in terms of what He says Christ did for you, how valuable you are, and who He has made you to be.

Another major hindrance to our maturing in Christ is the need for approval. Sin created a separation between God and man. Jesus, through the cross, reconciled man to God. As a result, we have God's acceptance and approval and do not need man's approval. This is called the doctrine of reconciliation.

Sometimes, because of the way they see themselves, when people fail, they blame themselves or punish others. In reality, Christ's substitutionary death on the cross paid the penalty for our sin, and He gave us His righteousness as a bonus. Therefore, there is no blame that can be given to us or anyone else. Whom can we blame or hold accountable for sins when Jesus has redeemed them? How can I blame myself when Jesus has forgiven me? To do so devalues Christ's accomplishment on the cross. You don't want to do that, do you? Then you have to accept what God says and accept that we have been made righteous because Jesus gave us His holy righteousness and took our filthy rags upon the cross. What love and what freedom!

Shame arises out of a negative evaluation of our past performance or a critical opinion of our physical appearance. The result of shame is a sense of worthlessness and hopelessness. God's answer to this problem is regeneration. When you are regenerated, a new you is created by the Holy Spirit. There is nothing negative about the new you. In fact, you are made perfect through regeneration. Because of your faith in Christ, He has made you into a new person. God created this new person from nothing. You have a brand-new nature with new potential and new capacities. You must agree with God and begin to see yourself as this new creation.

Romans 6:1-11, teaches us this truth – that we died with Christ and are resurrected with Him unto new life. Sin no longer has spiritual or legal power over us. *For we know that our old self was crucified with him so that the body of sin might be done away with, that we should no longer be slaves to sin* (Romans 6:6). *The New Spirit Filled Life Bible* commentary explains: "The body of sin refers to the sinful nature within us, not to the human body. The Greek verb translated done away with does not mean to become extinct, but to be defeated or deprived of power."[22]

In other words, Christ defeated the power sin once had over the body. As believers, although we struggle with sin, it no longer has power over us. Christians "have died to the love of sin and the ruling power of sin."[23] However, we are not yet dead to all of its influences. It is up to us to daily crucify the flesh and not allow sin to reign in our bodies. Your new spiritual self (the redeemed one) resides in your body right along with your old soul self (the unrighteous one). They are at war with one another. In order to bring the old you into line with the new you, Romans 12:2 tells us: ...*be transformed by the renewing of your mind.* In other words, study the Word of God, meditate on it and begin to put it in action in your life. Your mind, will, and emotions will begin to come into agreement with God and with the new you, as you *do* the Word, and the flesh loses its influence.

If you struggle with the areas mentioned here, I suggest you do an in-depth study on the above doctrines and come into agreement with God concerning them. As you align your old nature, found in your mind, will, and emotions, with the Word of God, you will experience peace, satisfaction and abundant living. This requires God's grace at work in your life; however, it also requires intentional effort on your part, so you have to really want it. Significance and worth are found only in Christ Jesus! There is no greater worth than to be so valuable that the One who is more valuable than all would die for you. He determined your life to be worth His life. As you align your thoughts with God's thoughts about you, you will develop a new kind of self-esteem. You might call it God-esteem. God declared you righteous and your worth is that of a child of God and royal priest of God. You were chosen by God because He loves you. Why run to other people in search of significance? He said you are of supreme worth. He has given you the most valuable purpose for your life. He is glorified in your acceptance of this revealed truth.

If you want to come into the fullness of the destiny God has planned for you, you must break the habit of using possessions, people, performance, and the judgments from others or yourself as your standard of evaluation. Begin using God's truth for your standard. Proverbs 23:7 says, *For as a man thinks, so he is.* Memorize and meditate on who God says you are. Get into agreement with God and your thought life will change. Watch out for your tongue. The words you speak about yourself should be the same words God speaks concerning you. Daily tell yourself and your Christian friends who you are in Christ. Any thought that is contrary to God's Word concerning you is a lie. Ask the Holy Spirit to help you identify the lies that trouble you. Then find God's answer – His truth that eradicates the lie. Memorize these truths and when the lies try to enter your mind, take them captive to the obedience of Christ (2 Corinthians 10:5). Guard your mind with the truth found in Scripture concerning who you are as a new creation in Christ!

The more truth you have in your mind, the easier it is for you to discern the lies of the one that comes to *steal, kill,* and *destroy.* The affirmation of God's love and acceptance will help you come into agreement with God. You will receive a new self-image. Accept all the things in your life you cannot change. Accept how God has fashioned you and who He made you to be. Determine today to begin defining your life by who you are in Christ!

Again, I caution you to guard yourself from allowing things to rob you of your true identity in Christ. I am reminded of my last trip to Nashville, Tennessee. We toured the Music Hall of Fame. It was amazing to look at Elvis Presley's car. The car that belonged to the King of Rock and Roll sported a 24kt gold and crushed diamond paint job. Few people in his time made as much money and acquired as much fame as he. It appeared that he had it all—money, airplanes, cars, mansions, fame, good looks, and talent. Yet he died at age 42, on an overdose of pills, after fighting serious bouts of depression. Things—they did not bring Elvis genuine satisfaction and they won't bring it to us either. Why have our identity wrapped up in them?

Accept all the things in your life you cannot change. Accept how God has fashioned you and who He made you to be. Determine today to begin defining your life by who you are as a new creation in Christ!

Moments at the Fountain

Reflection & Application

Things to Remember

- Those who walk in genuine satisfaction know and accept who they are as a new creation in Christ.

- You are valuable. Christ determined your life to be worth His.

- When God's Word is your standard of evaluation, your thinking transforms and you become satisfied.

- To experience real satisfaction, we must accept the truth of grace found in the gospel of Jesus Christ, for our salvation and concerning its affect on our life in the here and now.

2 Corinthians 5:17

Therefore, if anyone is in Christ, he is a new creation; the old has gone, the new has come!

1 Peter 2:9 (MSG)

But you are the ones chosen by God, chosen for the high calling of priestly work, chosen to be a holy people, God's instruments to do his work and speak out for him, to tell others of the night-and-day difference he made for you.

See Appendix B for a list of "Identity Scriptures"
to help grow your awareness of who you really are.

Reflect & Grow

1. Think about and identify the lies of the enemy that are embedded in your belief system? Then find the truth that eradicates that lie. For example: Romans 5:1 eliminates fear of failure. Write the truth(s) on a 3x5 card and when the lie comes to your mind, refuse to meditate upon it but instead speak the Word of God to it. Share some of these with one another if you are in a group.

2. Why is it that although we have been saved, we continue to struggle with sin? Discuss the application of Romans 12:2.

3. What can we do when we sin? Read 1 John 1:9.

4. How can we prevent devaluing ourselves when we sin?

5. What lie results in feelings of shame? What Bible doctrine can you use to eradicate that lie?

6. What lie is eradicated by the doctrine of reconciliation?

7. Are you on the performance merry-go-round? What can you do to get off of it and begin to experience contentment with who Christ has made you?

8. Why must you know who you are in Christ in order to experience satisfaction?

9. What does God call our failure to agree with Him concerning who He says we are; what He has called us to do; and how He will enable us to be obedient?

10. What are the two kinds of self esteem discussed in this chapter? Explain the difference between the two.

11. Explain how satisfaction increases with the realization that God made you significant and has given you purpose.

Prayer

Thank You, Father, for choosing me for the high calling of priestly work and to be Your witness and mouthpiece on earth. Thank You for freeing me from the bondage of sin. Help me to know and live in the reality of a new creation in Christ that You may be glorified in and through my life. In Jesus' name, I pray.

Confession

I am a loved child of the one true God – chosen and called to reign with Christ. I am righteous because He has made me righteous. His life has given my life significance and value because His life of infinite worth was given as payment for mine.

Chapter 12 ─────────────────────────
Reflecting Christ

And we, who with unveiled faces all reflect the Lord's glory,
are being transformed into His likeness with ever-increasing
glory, which comes from the Lord, who is the Spirit.
2 Corinthians 3:18

We are created in the image of God to glorify Him as we reflect Christ through our lives; but, how is it that we do this? As we reflect Christ in what we say and do, the world sees Christ's life through ours, and He is glorified. But glorifying God is more than living a religious life. It involves enjoying God through our lives as we walk in His ways through the events of our lives. *The Westminster Catechism* states the chief end of man is to glorify God by enjoying Him forever.[24] I see too many long-faced Christians walking through life as though living the Christian life is a joy-stealer. Something is lacking in one's relationship – either there is no real relationship or there is a lack of knowledge of the fullness of the Gospel – if a person who calls them self a Christian is not experiencing enjoyment in their relationship with God. Our joy, happiness and satisfaction seen in the midst of our valleys and mountain top experiences witnesses Christ's faith and life to others.

Real and lasting joy, happiness and satisfaction are cultivated in a believer's life as we walk through life's good and bad times and grow in Christ-likeness. These spiritual virtues are evidence of our spiritual maturity and are an internal matter expressed through our attitudes and seen in our behavior. Although the three are similar, each has a unique development and expression.

Joy means delight. In Nehemiah 8:20 we read that *the joy of the Lord is our strength*. The narrative surrounding this verse tells us that the people were convicted of their sin while hearing the law read. They began to mourn and weep. Nehemiah tells them to stop weeping and to celebrate what the Lord has done for them, for within the law was the provision for their sin. He encouraged them to celebrate the provision God made for their sins, through sacrifices, and be joyful about their redemption.

How many times do we focus on our sin, and its consequences, instead of Christ and His provision? This focus only leads to feelings of guilt, depression and hopelessness. God says *refocus* and *celebrate* what Jesus has done. Be *joyful* about your redemption! He has made provision for you. In addition to paying the legal debt required by God for our sin, He made provision for forgiveness of our sin on a daily basis. This means that when we mess up and sin after conversion, there is a way to be restored into fellowship with our God. Meanwhile, Jesus is at work in us, on a continual basis, breaking us free from the strangleholds that bind us. Our focus needs to be on Him. As we celebrate the Lord's sacrifice for our sins, rejoicing and delighting in it, we are strengthened to live through our life events – the failures, the pain, the trials, the temptations and to live in the holy liberty Christ makes available to us. We can walk out life knowing we are forgiven and have a sure redemption in Christ.

The joy of the Lord set before Christ, strengthening Him to endure the cross, was you and me, and our joy. Now we can receive strength for our trials as we find our joy in Christ who is set before us and who Himself is our reward for any suffering we endure as those who belong to Him. We can also rejoice knowing that as we share in His sufferings on earth, we will also share in His glory in eternity (Philippians 3:10-11). We remind ourselves this life is temporary – like smoke, it vanishes. But we have an eternal hope in Christ that promises us a glorious future without end.

Now our joy of the Lord – our delight in Him – should be displayed outwardly for others to see as we rejoice in Him and praise Him in every situation and circumstance. We recognize God for who He is… a God of love and salvation. Jesus said in Luke 10:20, *…rejoice that your names are written in heaven.* You see, we have reason to celebrate God whether we like our circumstances today or not. We rejoice in the Lord because we delight in belonging to Christ, while looking forward to the eternal hope we have in Him beyond this life. Rejoice in Christ and you will be strengthened!

Whereas, joy speaks of a knowledge regarding the provision that has been made for our sins (it is about our eternal hope in Christ Jesus), genuine *happiness* is a by-product of our devotion and obedience to God. It is a by-product of godliness. We see this as we read each Beatitude in Matthew 5, which states, *blessed or happy is the man who...* does a particular thing or who has cultivated a particular attitude, godly discipline, or behavior in his life. So, happiness is about cultivating godly disciplines and obedience to the Lord. It is advantageous to our spiritual development to study the Beatitudes and cultivate these godly attitudes for living life. You may want to read my book, *Experience Godliness God's Way* to deepen your understanding of the Beatitudes and God's way of cultivating godliness within His children.

Although joy, happiness and satisfaction are intricately interwoven and born out of our relationship with Christ, *satisfaction* is the fruit we specifically experience as we trust and accept God's rule in our lives. So, to be satisfied in Christ, you must be content knowing God is in control and you're not. You trust He has a good, loving purpose for all that goes on in your life. And, you realize His ways are higher than yours. You accept that your knowledge is limited. You realize there is much more to be revealed to you in your eternal future. And, you accept that your finite mind cannot possibly comprehend all of God's infinite ways. Even though you may not like what is going on or understand it, when you trust God has a perfect and eternal purpose in all things, you are able to maintain satisfaction. Yet, you know you are a stranger in a foreign land, a sojourner passing through earth on your way to your eternal home (Hebrews 11:13).

So, just as creation longs for Christ's return, so do believers yearn for that day they will meet Christ face to face. Meanwhile, our inner self longs for Him and His courts (Psalm 84:2). You see, unending satisfaction without lapse will not be found until we are dwelling with the Lord in heaven. Our souls are homesick while our hearts expectantly wait for Christ to return (Philippians 3:20).

There are times we get a taste of Christ – for example, in a worship service when we experience a glimpse of God's glory. There are also times we hear His voice intimately speaking to our spirit through Scripture and we are satisfied. These moments are fulfilling, yet at the same time, can make us homesick to be with our Father. Paul speaks of our hearts awaiting Christ's return with an expectant hope. Our hope is not without basis. Jesus promises us in John 14:2-3 that He will come again and we will join Him in the place He is preparing for us. Heaven will be beyond our wildest dreams. We will be at home and we will be so satisfied. First Corinthians 2:9 says, … *No eye has seen, no ear has heard, no mind has conceived what God has prepared for those who love him.*

While we await ultimate, unhindered satisfaction (available only when Christ returns for us or we go to Him), there is still hope for peace and *real* satisfaction; but again, it is just a taste of what is to come. David declared in Psalm 17:15: *And I – in righteousness I will see your face; when I awake, I will be satisfied with seeing your likeness.* Meanwhile on earth, we must continually put forth effort to spend time with God and be filled with His love. We must be intentional to commune with Him daily through worship, prayer and Scripture. Otherwise, our wells run dry as we go about the responsibilities and challenges we incur on our life's journey.

First Timothy 6:6 declares: *Godliness with contentment is great gain.* This is the pathway to the abundant life. There is no other. *Real* satisfaction is found only with the one who has a reverence for God and is pursuing Him while content trusting Him with their destiny and the things they cannot change. When the enemy tries to rob you of satisfaction by reminding you of sins you have laid at the cross and, therefore, been forgiven of, remember Christ, and that He gave His life to make provision for your sin. Be thankful and allow your joy to overflow and be your strength to continue the journey, content in Christ. Praise God and commune with Him often. In Psalm 63:5, David said that it was in *praising and intimate communion* with God that he felt satisfied. Won't you praise and seek Him today? As you do, He will draw near to you. There in His presence, He will fill you with His love and you will discover how life at the Fountain of Living Waters (God – your source for all you need) satisfies the longings of your soul.

Moments at the Fountain

Reflection & Application

Things to Remember

- We can be satisfied daily by pursuing God as we await the ultimate state of contentment to be experienced when we meet Him face to face.

- Joy speaks of a knowledge and acceptance of the provision Christ made for our sins – Look what the Lord has done!

- Satisfaction speaks of our intimacy with God and acceptance of His sovereign rule in our lives.

- Genuine happiness is a spiritual virtue and is a by-product of our devotion and obedience to God.

Psalm 17:15

And I – in righteousness I will see your face; when I awake, I will be satisfied with seeing your likeness.

Psalm 63:2-5

I have seen you in the sanctuary
and beheld your power and your glory.
Because your love is better than life,
my lips will glorify you.
I will praise you as long as I live,
and in your name I will lift up my hands.
I will be fully satisfied as with the richest of foods;
with singing lips my mouth will praise you.

1 Timothy 6:6
Godliness with contentment is great gain.

Reflect & Grow

1. Discuss how joy/rejoice, happiness and satisfaction are intertwined and how they differ?

2. In addition to God's children, what else is longing for redemption? Read Romans 8:22-23.

3. What is our life on earth like according to 2 Corinthians 5:4?

4. What are some things we can know about heaven? Read Revelation 21:4 and 22:3.

5. Explain how you can be satisfied on your life's journey while at the same time hunger for the fulfillment of your hope in Christ?

6. What are we to hunger and thirst for while journeying on the earth? Read Matthew 6:33.

7. Pray for God to stir up a hunger and thirst for Him and His ways.
   Here are some Scriptures to help:
   Psalm 42:2
   Psalm 107:9

8. How does it help you to experience satisfaction today as you think upon the truth of redemption and that the day is approaching that you will meet Jesus face to face?

9. Are you more satisfied today than you were at the beginning of this study? If in a group, share your experience and how God has worked within you.

10. Make a commitment to continue to learn and grow in satisfaction. If in a study group, perhaps you can hold one another accountable in your commitment to God in the weeks ahead by occasionally asking one another, "Are you satisfied with the life God has given you today?"

Prayer

Father, I praise You for the life You have given me and the honor to live in Your presence as your child. Thank You for always bringing me through the good times and the bad. Thank You that You are changing me and perfecting me. Thank You for guarding my heart and mind, and for giving me Your perspective on life. I rejoice as I look forward to the day I will stand face to face with You in all Your glory experiencing the fullness of satisfaction in the fullness of Your presence. Meanwhile, I ask You to continue to stir a hunger up in my soul for more of You and to satisfy me with Your unfailing love. Thank You for blessing me with Your favor and the happiness that results from living my life in You. Be glorified, Lord, as the line between where I end and You begin lessens. In Your name, I pray.

Confession

By the grace of God and a surrendered life to the Holy Spirit and Word of God, I am being changed from the inside out – growing in godliness and contentment each day. I am overcoming by the blood of the lamb and the word of my testimony. I am satisfied and experiencing the abundant life found in relationship with Christ, while I await that glorious day of Christ's appearance as the King of Kings and Lord of Lords.

A Final Thought

Remember the Wisdom in the

Book of Ecclesiastes

As you walk out this journey of satisfaction, remember the wisdom found in the Book of Ecclesiastes where the minister after a change of heart realized life did have meaning after all. He discovers satisfaction is available for you who are in relationship with God as you:

1. Learn to explore life by faith (11:1-6);

2. Enjoy life with a knowledge of God's goodness as Creator and His righteousness as Judge (11:7-12:8);

3. Learn lessons from life's events, recognizing your human limitations and getting a God perspective on things (12:9-12);

4. Treat life as a possession over which God has given you stewardship fearing God and walking in reverence and obedience to Him (12:13-14).

Remember, life is a journey and real satisfaction is learned as you draw strength from Christ for every season and trial. Spend time with God as your Source for everything. I pray that you will enjoy life and enjoy God along your journey to satisfaction and abundant living.

Appendix A

Understanding the How of
Salvation

*He who has the Son has the life; he who does not
have the Son of God does not have the life.*

1 John 5:12

*T*he Bible says, *...the gift of God is eternal life through Jesus Christ our Lord* (Romans 6:23). Heaven is a gift and like any gift, it is not earned and it is given even though not deserved. You could not do enough good deeds to earn a place in heaven. Ephesians 2:8, 9 says, *For by grace are you saved through faith; and not of yourselves: it is the gift of God: not of works, lest any man should boast.* You may ask why it is that no one can earn his way to heaven. The answer is, All have sinned and come short of the glory of God (Romans 3:23). Everyone has transgressed God's law with the sin or sin(s) of lying, lust, cheating, deceit, evil thoughts, immoral behavior and more. So man is unable to save himself. He cannot be good enough. Matthew 5:48 tells us, *Be ye therefore perfect, even as your Father which is in heaven is perfect.* Neither you nor I can meet this standard. However, in spite of our sin God in His mercy has loved us. *...I have loved thee with an everlasting love....* (Jeremiah 31:3). *God is love* according to 1 John 4:8 and He does not want to punish us. But God is also just and therefore He must punish sin. He says, *... (I) will by no means clear the guilty....* (Exodus 34:7) and *...the soul that sinneth, it shall die* (Ezekiel 18:4). So God had this problem of loving us and not wanting to punish us; yet being a just and holy God He must punish sin. He solved this problem for us through Jesus Christ. The Bible tells us clearly that He is the infinite God-man. *In the beginning was the Word (Jesus)...and the Word (Jesus) was God. And the Word (Jesus) was made flesh, and dwelt among us....* (John 1:1, 14) So Jesus Christ came to earth and lived a perfect and sinless life. Then He died on the cross to pay the penalty of our sins and rose from the grave to purchase a place for us in heaven. *All we like sheep have gone astray; we have turned every one to his own way; and the LORD hath laid on Him (Jesus) the transgressions (sin) of us all* (Isaiah 53:6). Jesus Christ bore our sin in His body on the cross and now offers you eternal life (heaven) as a free gift.

To receive this free gift, you must have saving faith. Saving faith is not mere intellectual assent, like believing certain historical facts. The Bible says the devil believes there is one God, so believing there is one God is not saving faith. Saving faith is not mere temporal faith either. It is not trusting God in a temporary crisis situation such as financial, family or for some physical need. These are things we can trust God for, but they are not saving faith!

Saving faith is trusting Jesus Christ alone for eternal life. It means resting upon Christ alone and what He has done rather than in what you or I have done to get us into heaven. *...Believe (trust) on the Lord Jesus Christ and thou shalt be saved....* (Acts 16:31). This is the greatest story ever told about the greatest offer ever made by the greatest person who ever lived, Jesus Christ.

The question now is, would you like to receive Jesus Christ—the gift of eternal life? To do this you need to transfer your trust from what you have been doing to Christ on the cross and accept Christ as Savior by opening your heart and inviting Him in. He says, *Behold, I stand at the door, and knock: if any man hears My voice, and opens the door, I will come in to him....* (Revelation 3:20).

Receive Jesus Christ as Lord of your life by giving Him the driver's seat and control of your life—not the back seat.

Repent by turning from anything that is not pleasing to Him. He will reveal His will to you as you grow in your relationship with Him.

Now if this is what you really want you can go to God in prayer right where you are. You can receive His gift of eternal life through Jesus Christ right now. *For with the heart man believes unto righteousness; and with the mouth confession is made unto salvation. For whosoever shall call upon the name of the Lord shall be saved* (Romans 10:10, 13). If you want to receive the gift of eternal life through Jesus Christ, then call on Him, asking Him for this gift right now. Here's a suggested prayer: "Lord Jesus Christ, I know I am a sinner and do not deserve eternal life. But, I believe You died and rose from the grave to purchase a place in heaven for me. Lord Jesus, come into my life; take control of my life; forgive my sins and save me. I repent of my sins and now place my trust in You for my salvation. I accept the free gift of eternal life."

If this prayer is the sincere desire of your heart, look at what Jesus promises to those who believe in Him: Verily, verily, I say unto you, he that believeth on Me hath everlasting life (John 6:47 KJV).

Welcome to God's family! *But as many as received Him, to them gave He power to become the sons of God, even to them that believe on His name* (John 1:12 NKJV).[25]

You now belong to God and if you have surrendered your life to Him, you are in the best hands you can be in– His hands! Now you can continue on in your search for satisfaction with an expectation to discover it!

Appendix B
Identity Scriptures for the Christian:
Who You Really Are

*S*eek to know the real you...the one whom God has called you to be. God has identified who you really are. Call yourself by the following...

2 Corinthians 5:17
A new Creation in Christ Jesus.

John 1:12
God's child

John 15:15
Christ's friend

Romans 5:1
Justified

Colossians 1:14
Redeemed and forgiven of all my sins

Romans 8:17
An heir of God in Christ Jesus

Ephesians 2:10
God's workmanship created to do good works which He has prepared for me

2 Corinthians 5:21

The righteousness of God in Christ Jesus. Reigning in life
by Christ Jesus through the abundance of grace and the
gift of righteousness... and I am a king and priest unto God

1 Peter 2:9

A royal priesthood, a holy nation, a person for God's
own possession

1 Corinthians 6:17

United with the Lord and one spirit with Him

1 Corinthians 6:19, 20

Purchased with a price by God

1 Corinthians 12:27

A member of Christ's body

Ephesians 1:5

Adopted by God as a child of God

Ephesians 1:1

A saint

Ephesians 2:18

Able to access God directly through the Holy Spirit

Colossians 2:10

Complete in Christ

Ephesians 2:10

God's workmanship

Ephesians 3:12

Confident and free to approach God at any time

Romans 8:1 & 2 Timothy 1:7

Free from condemnation and the spirit of fear

2 Timothy 1:7

Filled with a spirit of power, love and sound, disciplined mind

Romans 8:37 & 1 John 5:4

A conqueror and a world overcomer

Ephesians 1:3

Blessed with every spiritual blessing

Philippians 4:19

Free from want and lack, for God has liberally supplied my every need

John 15:5

A branch of the vine and I bear much fruit

1 Corinthians 3:16 & 6:19

A temple of God and the Holy Spirit dwells in me

Romans 8:1, 2

Free of condemnation

Romans 8:35

Assured of the love of God and nothing can separate me from it

Romans 8:28

Assured God works all things in my life together for good

Philippians 3:20

A citizen of heaven

1 John 4:4

Indwelt by the Greater One and I have overcome the evil one

Galatians 3:13

Redeemed from the curse of the law

3 John 2

Prospering and in exceeding abundant health as my
soul is prospering

Ephesians 4:24

Created in righteousness and true holiness

1 Corinthians 15:58

Steadfast, unmovable, always abounding in the work
of the Lord

Acts 13:52

Continually filled with joy and the Holy Spirit

2 Peter 2:24 & Is 53:5

Healed by the stripes of Jesus and free from pain in my body

Romans 8:31

Free from guilt charges against me

2 Corinthians 1:21, 22

Established, anointed and sealed by God

Colossians 3:3

Hidden with Christ in God

Philippians 3:20

Being perfected by God

2 Timothy 1:7

Free of fear, Sound in mind possessing a spirit of
power and love

Hebrews 4:16

A recipient of God's grace and mercy in my times of need

Ephesians 6:14

Standing and acting on the truth of God's Word

Ephesians 4:29

Speaking words of faith, which edify and minister grace to the hearer

2 Corinthians 5:20 & Romans 8:14

An Ambassador for Christ Jesus and I am led by the Holy Spirit

2 Corinthians 5:7

Walking by Faith and not by sight

2 Peter 1:4

A partaker of God's divine nature and have escaped the corruption of the world

2 Corinthians 2:14

Always triumphant in Christ Jesus

1 Corinthians 15:57

Always having and living in victory through my Lord Jesus Christ

John 15:16

Chosen and appointed to bear fruit

2 Corinthians 5:17

A minister of reconciliation for God

2 Corinthians 6:1 & 1 Corinthians 3:9

God's co-worker

Matthew 5:13-14

The salt of the earth, the light of the world

Isaiah 54:14

Far from oppression and fear; and terror shall not come near me

Psalm 1:3

A tree of righteousness which yields much fruit and
is prospering

Philippians 4:6-7

Free from anxiety and care

Ephesians 6:10

Strong in the Lord and the power of His might

Ephesians 2:6

Seated with Christ in the heavenly realm

Philippians 4:13

Can do all things through Christ who strengthens me

Acts 1:8

A personal witness of Christ

Leader's Guide for Chapter Reflection Questions

---

*T*his study guide has been included to answer and supplement the answers to the questions found at the end of each chapter. In many cases, the answers here include additional comments that are not found in the chapter itself, so please be sure to compare what is here with each question of each week's lesson. In your preparation time, it is a good idea to discover the answers for yourself through prayer and review of the chapter and then read the notes in this guide. You may want to prioritize the questions, once you have done the lesson, in order of importance. Some meetings may not have time to answer every question and some questions will require more time than others. Some questions may appear to be a repeat, yet the answers shown here will reveal a different principle or truth that was intended to be discovered. Do not hesitate to share what God shares with you concerning the weekly topic. If you are a Christian, you have the same Holy Spirit dwelling within you that I do. God is always revealing things to us and He may share something with you, a Scripture, illustration, or a short testimony, that may help the members to make application of the principle in their own lives. Begin your personal preparation time with prayer and encourage others to do so as well. Also, do not forget to pray for the members of your group and for their desire and level of commitment to be unwavering. You will find that some do all the work each week; whereas, others do none or little. Of course, personal study always helps the material to take root within us, but the study is such that those who do not do the questions for whatever reason, can still gain from the study if they commit to read and attend each meeting. Pray for the time spent together to set everyone on course for a deeper relationship with God and a life testifying of spiritual growth with contentment. The weekly reading time for most chapters for most people is estimated to be 15 to 20 minutes/week so most people can do this. Some chapters do have additional Scriptures to look up and consider. Of course, for those who do so, their knowledge of God and the blessing of living satisfied in Christ is sure to go deeper than those who do not take the time to dig for the treasure found in the Word of God. As a springboard into your discussion, you may want to do an icebreaker followed by asking the members to share the truth or principle they learned or were reminded of that had the greatest impact for them from the week's reading. And, remember, personal opinions and experiences are welcome, however, God's Word is the standard we want to take as truth for our lives. It is the only truth that sets us free to live a happy, satisfied, abundant life.

Chapter One - Leader's Guide

1. Personal assessment. Suggest members retake this assessment at the end of the study to see how their thinking has changed as well as to see the difference in the level of satisfaction they are experiencing from now to then.

2. See page 16 for similarities. You may want to give some specific examples to this question of what is currently going on in the world, country, your community or other areas of your life that pertain to any of the areas listed here: crooked politics, incompetent leadership, guilty people getting away with doing wrong, people wishing for the "the good ole days." From generation to generation we hear of these same issues and it appears there is nothing one can do to improve life or find any purpose in it (all is meaningless). However, if we include God in life's equation, considering life from the standpoint of God's character, His love, His power, His purpose, and His only begotten Son and His sacrifice made for us, we find purpose, meaning and satisfaction.

3. The answer is 'yes.' You may want to give a personal example or an example from someone's life you know. Goals are good when they are a result of our relationship with God; however, we must maintain a thankful attitude where we are at present while we are on our way to where God is taking us. We can be thankful knowing He has purpose in our present situation and that He is with us in it.

   I believe in goal setting for every area of our life: body, soul (mind, will, emotions) and spirit. Goals help us to measure progress and progress is important to God (Scripture speaks of us growing), therefore, He has created us such that we are more content as we progress forward toward the goals we establish with God's direction. Remember, contentment is ACTIVE. Those who are content will be found: Following Christ/obeying God; Learning/growing in knowledge of God; Testifying/witnessing Christ; and, Serving/the work of ministry. It stands to reason we would have goals in these areas. We know that if we are seeking God to impart His desires to us, that He will fulfill those desires through us in His perfect timing (Psalm 37:4). Goals given us through our relationship with God help us to maximize progress and progress feeds contentment. Satisfaction is not complacency. It is active, not passive.

4. Paul experienced a total change of lifestyle as a Christian in comparison to his life before Christ revealed Himself to him: He was persecuted, beaten, stoned, left for dead, put on trial, imprisoned, ship-wrecked. Also, read 2 Corinthians 11:22-30; 2 Corinthians 12:7: (1) Satisfaction is imparted to us through our relationship with God (Psalm 145:16). (2) It is learned through the circumstances of life as we learn to draw upon the strength of Christ in them

(Philippians 4:11-13). All who live godly – who live with an attitude of piety (devotion and reverence) towards God, will suffer some kind of persecution (2 Timothy 3:12). Paul's only concern was the exaltation of Christ through his life whether that came from his death, or through his life, mattered not to him. He even considered death as profitable in that He would be with the Lord. He knew wisdom, provision and strength for life's situations was found in Christ and not himself. Therefore, he depended on the grace of God (God's strength and provision) and thereby, learned contentment (Philippians 4:11-13). When we make the glory of Christ our main goal, as did Paul, all else will pale in the light of it, and have no power to rob us of our satisfaction. We trust Christ for what He will do living through us because we live as ONE with Him. We say, "I can't do this Lord. I ask that you do this through me that you may be glorified through this situation. Your Kingdom come, Your will be done."

5. He asks for love. He says receiving love will result in his satisfaction. Prayer: God, I ask you and thank you to fill and satisfy my soul with your love.

6. Contentment comes from pursuing motivating and desirable goals imparted through our relationship with God. Therefore, without Christ, life has no meaning or purpose. Nothing satisfies as man's desires are insatiable when they are not flowing from God and filled by God. Viewing life without God, results in hopelessness as we live and we die all the while dissatisfied. With Christ, life is eternal and has purpose in the here and now as well as for all eternity. We were made for God. He is the source of our life and the only one who can satisfy us.

7. Complacency is passive; contentment is active. Increase in our knowledge of God (pray and study the Scriptures), intentionally remind ourselves concerning the things of God (Israelites built memorials to help them do this) and make our calling and election sure with effectiveness and productiveness in our knowledge of Christ (increase in our measure of the qualities found in 2 Peter 1:5-7). *Draw near to God and He will draw near to you* (James 4:8).

8. When we view life and its circumstances without considering God's character, and power, we are viewing life from below the sun (without an eternal perspective). When we view circumstances and life considering His power, purpose and plan, we are viewing life from above the sun. To say it another way: If we apply our limited human reasoning to the complexities and challenges of life, we are viewing life from under the sun. When we apply to life God's reasoning, as found in Scripture, we view life from above the sun. Learning to view life from God's perspective requires focused training in godliness (1 Tim 4:7-8). For more about training in godliness, you may want to check out these two books: *Experience Godliness God's Way* and *Enjoying God Through Purposeful Living: An Exercise in the Spiritual Disciplines*.

9. God gives things to us for our enjoyment (1 Timothy 6:17). We should pursue God and allow Him to give us the things we need and desire. If we seek other things as a substitute for God, we will be disappointed and find their fulfillment will quickly flee. See last paragraph of page 17 and first part of page 18 for a review on this topic. God is to be the source of our desires and the source for their fulfillment.

10. The abundant life is found in living life in Christ. As we, the branches, stay attached to Christ, the Vine, His love, power, strength, wisdom, desires – His life – flow into our life. We find that we have more than enough for every situation we find ourselves in. This is true abundance. 1 Timothy 6:6 declares: *godliness with contentment is great gain.*

11. Review page 19. Eve was on her way to deception when she considered the lie she was told that was in direct contradiction with what God had said. When we have a thought that does not agree with the Word of God, it is imperative that we replace the thought with the truth, to protect ourselves from deception. We can't do that if we do not know the truth. It is dangerous to think upon, consider, mull over an ungodly thought because it doesn't take long for it to take root into our belief system. Once Eve considered the lie that God was withholding something good from her, it took root producing a negative emotion which resulted in an ungodly attitude that led to ungodly behavior. Her decision to consider and then follow her emotions instead of the Word from God, led to chaos for all creation. Warning: Consideration of lies that appeal to our self-centeredness will lead to dissatisfaction and deception. This can then lead to ungodly decisions and behavior with negative effects for both our lives and the lives of others.

Chapter Two - Leader's Guide

1. Personal reflection. Ask the group if anyone wants to share. The Scripture calls this downward spiraling effect of ungodly desire a diluted heart. It can lead to dissatisfaction and a hardened heart towards God.

2. Idolatry is a sin against God. He is a jealous God, possessing a righteous jealousy, not a jealousy as we know it. His jealousy is a desire for what is best for us and He is what is best for us.

3. Idolatry equals possessing a desire for anything in heaven or on the earth beneath or in the waters below above one's desire for God. Anything that we revere or worship above God – that takes priority over God, His Kingdom and righteousness. If it takes us away from God or we depend on it as a source to

meet any need we have, then it is idolatry. We should guard ourselves from giving anything or anyone the place, the honor, the worship that belongs only to God. He is to be #1 in the hearts of His people.

4. Money in itself or things purchased with money do not satisfy. The question is: Why waste our time, energy, money or any of our resources seeking after that which only leaves us empty?

5. A failure to continue pursuing God after salvation. Salvation is a free gift but we must be intentional about pursuing God after we are saved if we are to experience real satisfaction.

6. In the presence of God.

7. Genuine satisfaction is available to those who are born again (belong to Christ) and who pursue godliness through an intentional relationship with Him.

8. Godliness with contentment is great gain (1Timothy 6:6).

9. It's a downward spiral eventually leading to death. Every man is the servant of the master to whose commands he yields himself; whether it be the sinful dispositions of his own heart, or in behavior which leads to death. The further down we travel on this spiral, the more difficult it is to find truth; and, be it not for the grace of God, one would not. There is no in between – either we are serving the master of death or the master of life. We can serve Christ, who gives life by the new and spiritual obedience implanted by regeneration.

10. It is experiencing God's unfailing love that satisfies our soul. As we spend time with Him and are filled with and comforted by His love, we are satisfied. As we experience Him (He is love) in the midst of our circumstances, we are satisfied. It is His 'unfailing' love that compels Him to work all things together for good to those who love Him and are called by Him. What contentment we find in His unfailing love. To spend time with God first thing in the morning prepares us with the benefit of remembering and experiencing His love before we begin to go about the challenges and distractions of our daily walk. This meeting with God enables us to walk through our day without losing our contentment.

Chapter Three - Leader's Guide

1. Personal reflection and answers. Thoughts that do not lead to faith in God should be discarded immediately and replaced with the promises of God. Last question in #1—Group members can share how we can apply Luke 19:10: *"For the Son of Man came to seek and save the lost"* to the challenge of changing the thought patterns in their thinking. The power of God is available to us to do all things through Christ. We have His presence in our lives available to help us if

we will just call out to Him, and quit trying to do it in our own strength. Another response might be: God put on flesh and came to earth to suffer and die that I may have life. That is a love I can trust. I can know that He has my best interest at the core of His being, while at the same time, I know there is nothing too difficult for Him. I can trust Him and rest because I am in His hands.

2. Listen to personal answers. You may hear answers that reflect the answer in the next question but to address the art of changing habits – we can become intentional and make the decision to pay attention to our thoughts so we can take them captive to the promises of God in Christ Jesus (2 Corinthians 10:5). Then we are able to go to God in prayer and release our worries. Also see Matthew 11:28-29.

3. It brings peace when we learn to release our worries to God and let Him take care of them. We do this as we follow the instruction found in Philippians 4:6 and 7: pray, petition with thanksgiving, make requests known to God; guard our hearts and minds with supernatural peace as we trust Him to work things out in His perfect time. A few other things that could be done include: making and carrying with you Scripture cards that are pertinent to your situation, joining in prayer with a close friend(s), speaking the promises of God.

4. God's peace that surpasses our natural understanding guards our hearts and minds. Again, we pray and petition Him with thanksgiving.

5. See page 40-43. (1) **Surrender** to God's purpose and plan. (2) **Trust** God's love and sovereign control over the affairs of your life. (3) **Focus** on the reality of eternity and your eternal rewards. Nothing, as good or bad as it may be, is greater than the promise we have in Christ. (4) **Pray and be thankful.** Prayer is first and foremost. Prayer produces peace and peace is a guard over our minds. Be thankful: Remember how the Lord has come through in the past. Remember your salvation. (5) **View** your present circumstances in light of the promises of God (6) **Speak aloud** the promises of God pertaining to your situation.

6. Comment: Knowing and understanding God, His love, sovereignty and ways results in trust in the character of God. When you have this trust, you will no longer feel the need to second guess God's responses to the events of your life.

7. Personal Question for private response.

8. Hebrews 11:6 – *And without faith it is impossible to please God, because anyone who comes to him must believe that he exists and that he rewards those who earnestly seek him.* Worry is unbelief. We see the results of unbelief throughout Scripture including the account of the twelve spies that went to check out the situation in the land God had promised to give to the Israelites.

Only two of the twelve came back encouraging the people to go forward and take the land, declaring the promise of God to give it to them. The other ten insisted in not moving forward. God judged the sin of the unbelief of the ten spies and the Israelites agreement with them to trust their natural eye instead of trusting in the character of God, with 40 years of wandering in the desert. Also, all those over the age of twenty died in the desert, never to see the promised land.

9. One point you may want to bring out after the group shares is the promise of Romans 8:28-29. This promise, when believed, brings peace to our minds. God certainly is in control (Isa 45:6,7; 43:13).

10. The opposite of faith is sight. The opposite of fear is love. Love activates our faith and energizes it (Galatians 5:6). See page 45 and 46.

11. Personal answers are to be shared voluntarily. 2 Timothy 1:7 tells us (1) Fear is a spirit (2) God does not give us a spirit of fear (3) God gives a spirit of power, of love and of self-discipline. When we walk in fear, we are without power, lacking in love and self-discipline (our mind is unsound).

12. Love is the opposite of fear. If you have a spirit of fear, you do not have the spirit of love. We must grow in our knowledge of God's character in order to increase faith and eliminate fear. You may have some fear, but not a fear that paralyzes and usurps control over you. Without a knowledge of God's character, we will constantly second guess God's responses to our life challenges.

13. Possible answer: It reminds me that no matter what is going on, I can rejoice knowing that my salvation is in Christ. There are many things out of my control, but just as my eternal salvation was not a problem for Christ, nothing I am facing right now or will ever face is a problem for Him. Besides, God gave Christ up for me. Scripture declares: Will He not then give me all things? I can trust God and there is always hope for those who are Christ's. You may also want to read and comment on Romans 8:35-39.

Chapter Four - Leader's Guide

1. The world's view of satisfaction is to do what makes you feel good for the moment without considering God. It teaches that satisfaction comes from external things such as people, positions, awards, and things. It involves the possessing indulging, hoarding and obtaining of something outside of one's self.

2. It feeds us with marketing efforts designed to feed our self-centered natures, bombarding us with TV, Internet and billboard ads promising happiness. They attempt to focus our attention on ourselves to the degree that we become dissatisfied and even depressed if we do not have whatever they are promoting.

3. One answer is: Keep your focus on Christ and eternal things. Guard your gateways to your heart, especially your sight and hearing. Pay attention to your thoughts and do not allow thoughts that lead to dissatisfaction roam your mind.

4. Contemplative question. Share your thoughts and listen to the thoughts of group members. Comment: There are times we all feel down or a little less than joyful, however, when we feel this way the majority of the time or a lot of the time, then we need to stop deceiving ourselves and others. Go to God and perhaps seek your Pastor's, or a Christian counselor's, or a friend's guidance.

5. You can instruct this question as a private matter with the group; or, you can ask the group to discuss this question, not necessarily from a personal stand-point, but from what they have seen as they have journeyed through life. Help the group to understand how to release their sin and accept God's love and forgiveness (1 John 1:9).

6. There could be several comments. Some may include: External sources, whether people or things, are all subject to change. When our faith is in them, we are disappointed when they change. Our internal source is God dwelling in us in the person of the Holy Spirit. God is the same yesterday, today and forever. It is much better to put our trust in Him. God lives in our spirit and as we pursue Him and His love, He satisfies us. His love is also eternal and He has given those Christ died for, eternal life.

7. Individual answers will apply here. Comment: It will take a committed decision and intentional effort to make the changes necessary by taking control of one's mind and actions.

8. Personal testimonies.

9. Again, nothing or no one can be 100% trusted. Everything else is subject to change except for God. Also, God created us for relationship with Himself. He placed a vacuum, so to speak, within us that can be filled only by Him. When all of our basic needs are met and we are dissatisfied, we can know it is a spiritual issue and we need to spend time with God.

10. When we pursue things instead of pursuing God, they will bring us grief. Many times they will lead us away from God and faith. However, if we pursue God and through that pursuit, God gives things to us, we will be able to enjoy what has been given as long as we continue to keep Him our #1 priority.

Chapter Five - Leader's Guide

1. Psalm 68 - (1) God goes before His chosen people when they are waiting on the promises of God to come to fruition in their lives, and when they cannot find their way in times of uncertainty, grief, distress, disappointment and wandering. He went out before Israel represented by the Ark of the Covenant during their 40 years of wandering in the desert before God brought them into the promised land of Canaan. (2) God is a powerful warrior for His people. (3) God blesses and refreshes His people in times of weariness. (4) God provides and makes a way for His people when in need or oppressed. Leviticus – Although Christ paid for our sin in full in regards to the legal debt owed to God, there are consequences for sin and for turning away from God individually and as a nation. However, God does not turn His back on His people, He gives correction for the purpose of getting the attention of His people and turning them back to Him. Genesis – God works what appears to us to be devastating circumstances for His own sovereign purpose and plan. Also seen in Romans 8:28.

    Deuteronomy 4:39 – God is in sovereign control of life's events. He hardens and softens hearts for His purposes. The world's kings (authorities and powers) are under God's control. Also see Proverbs 21:1. He has ultimate control over all including world politics. Exodus – God chooses to whom He will give mercy and show compassion. We are His creation. It is right and it is good.

    First Samuel – God is sovereign over all things. He has complete authority and power above everyone and everything. This is where we need to understand that God is also Love and He sheds His love abroad to us, giving us warning and many times warnings before His correction comes. Also, when negative things happen, it may not be a correction. Look at Jesus on the cross and Joseph sold into slavery and thrown into prison, Paul beat and eventually beheaded and on and on. God does all things for His purpose and plan of which we are not always privy of what that plan is.

2. Leviticus 26:40-43 – accept consequences of our sin and the punishment that results.

    Psalm 139:13-14 – accept ourselves as marvelous creations of God.

    Genesis 1:27 – accept that we are equal in worth and value of others.

    John 16:33— accept the good and bad circumstances of life.

    Psalm 68:7-10 – accept God's provision and power.

    1 Timothy 1:15-17 – accept Christ as Savior!

    Proverbs 3:5-6 – Accept that we may not understand the what or why God is doing or allowing a situation in our lives.

3. God is judge; struggles are opportunities for growth and we need to remember that God is with us giving us His strength to bring us through them.

4. This could be a personal reflection question; however, it would be advantageous if anyone wants to share how God has come through for them, and how He has delivered them from such things as drugs, a bad marriage, and parenting struggles, illness, relationship issues, fear, indecisiveness, abuse, emotional struggles, etc.

5. Personal reflection question to be done outside of the group while in prayer and communion with God. This is a great question to revisit periodically throughout our lives.

6. Acceptance of the things we cannot change, by the grace of God, is important if we are to be satisfied. I always think of the Serenity Prayer: Lord, help me accept the things I cannot change; courage to change the things I can (that need changed) and the wisdom to know the difference –

   Things we can change include: attitudes, priorities, what we do; habits, where we go, what we watch, etc. We cannot change someone else's actions, where we were born, natural physical traits (not including our weight), etc.

   You may want to ask if anyone would like to share a personal experience they are struggling with and help them identify if it is something out of their control, or is it something they can change. If it is out of their control, they must release it to God and trust Him in it. If it is something they can do something about, then help them as you are led by the Holy Spirit to make a plan to change the situation. Be careful not to spend too much time by giving them a time limit at the beginning.

7. Ask if anyone would like to share a personal experience. Again, these must be kept short. We can be influenced by people, television, internet, etc. We have to be careful to guard the gateways to our hearts – our five senses of hearing, seeing, touching, smelling, tasting, but especially hearing, seeing and touching. We also need to recognize the thoughts that come to our minds that are ungodly and take them captive to the obedience of Christ (2 Corinthians 10:5). This requires a firm decision to not allow thoughts that do not agree with God to roam around in the mind. If we fail to do this, and instead we meditate on the ungodly thought, ungodly emotions will attach to the thought and then an attitude will develop. At this point, we have a stronghold developing in our life and it will be seen in our behavior.

8. Everything we are and have is by the grace of God. He is our source for everything including satisfaction. He woos us to draw near to Him, and when we respond, He fills us with His love and satisfies our longings. It is all by His

grace. Satisfaction is imparted to us through our relationship with God. See Psalm 145:16.

9. Answers could include: Pray; Check for sin in one's own life and if God reveals something, repent and accept His forgiveness; maintain a thankful heart; relinquish control (don't try to fix it yourself) and accept God's plan in the situation; align attitudes with God's Word; trust God to work out His plan and purpose in His perfect timing.

10. Many times, Christians quote Romans 8:28 without the following verse, but the following verse should be considered with it if we are to get its full meaning. God's ultimate purpose is to mold us into the image of Christ. He works all things – not just the good things, not just some things – but all things together for those who love Him and are called (that's His children – Christians) towards this purpose. It will be finished when we meet Christ face-to-face (Romans 8:28-29).

Chapter Six - Leader's Guide

1. Many times we hurt due to not forgiving ourselves. Encourage the group members to forgive themselves. God through Christ has already forgiven those Christ died for. To withhold forgiveness when God has released forgiveness is setting oneself on a higher level than God. To withhold forgiveness is essentially saying that Christ's life, His blood poured out for your sin, does not carry a higher value than your sin. Nothing, even the sin of murder, can be compared to the value of the life of God. Follow the instructions in 1 John 1:9 and let it go. The same truth holds for those who have done wrong against you, whether intentionally or unintentionally. To hold them in unforgiveness is essentially setting yourself up as judge, a position that belongs only to Christ. To do this: Refocus attention on the cross. (1) Remember that Christ forgave you even when you were at enmity with Him (and He is God). He forgave you, even though you did not deserve to be forgiven. Therefore, you must forgive those who sin against you as well. This principle is powerfully explained in the parable found in Matthew 18:21-35. Christ forgave you and the one who hurt you (if they are a Christian), although He suffered beyond measure because of your and (their) sin. Ask yourself: Is your hurt of more value than His life? Is your hurt, as painful as it is, more traumatic than the persecution and suffering He experienced at the cross? With this in mind, (2) Release forgiveness to others and receive God's healing so you can live free (3) Still having trouble, ask Him to help you by forgiving them through you. Ask Him to change your heart.

2. It had been years since the Israelites had heard the Law read. As it was read, they were convicted of their sin and began to weep and mourn. Nehemiah told them to stop weeping and begin rejoicing because God had made provision for their sin (the animal sacrifice system). We should, indeed, repent for our sins when we are convicted by the Holy Spirit about them. However, we do not need to cling to them or focus on them. We should not continue weeping or worrying about them. Christ was the provision made for our sin, and unlike the atonement system of the Old Testament, Christ made atonement once and for all. It is finished. When we sin after our salvation, our instructions are to repent and receive God's cleansing and forgiveness (1 John 1:9). Repentance simply means, when the Holy Spirit reveals your sin, you admit it is sin, and you turn from it.

3. It is fine to have pride in our heritage to some degree. What we must guard against is putting more importance on that heritage than our heritage as a new creation in Christ, an adopted child of God. Paul declared that his heritage was nothing in comparison to His new heritage found in Christ (Philippians 3:5). Jesus also shows us that being a child in the family of God takes precedence over our natural earthly heritage (Matthew 12:46-50). We should treat one another in the body of Christ accordingly, as brothers and sisters for eternity.

4. God's plans are good and for our good. He desires for us to be hopeful knowing that He knows the future and has it in His control; and, He will bring us through even our most difficult and painful seasons. He sees the bigger picture while our perspective is limited.

5. Group members can share, as they are comfortable, how they themselves have experienced their faith in God in good and/or challenging times.

6. Jesus Christ is the same today as yesterday and will be the same tomorrow. This should give us confidence knowing that although people change, He does not. Sometimes people let us down but we can know that Christ's character and ways are constant. Sometimes men have lied to us, but we can count on Christ's faithfulness to His promises revealed to us in Scripture. He is not a man that lies or changes His perspective or ways.

7. Jesus sweat drops of blood when praying in the Garden of Gethsemane, asking God if there was another way to save us other than the way of the cross. Yet, He surrendered to the Father's sovereign wisdom and was strengthened in the knowledge of the purpose at hand. We can endure God's will in our lives when we are going through distressful times by surrendering to God and saying as Christ did, "Not my will but Yours be done." We do this for the sake of Christ and we do it by faith, believing God has good and perfect purpose in it. Read

Philippians 1:29-30 and 3:8-9. We persevere, relying on Christ's strength – not our own.

8. Trials result in steadfastness which results in perfecting us to the point that we lack no spiritual thing.

9. Personal reflection question. Yet, you might ask if anyone would like to share their personal experience with the group.

10. Jesus' joy was to fulfill the plan of God for our salvation no matter what it required of Him to do so. We are His joy as we were set before Him as His inheritance. He desired that just as His eyes were set on the eternal purpose and plan of God, instead of earthly rewards, benefits and circumstances, so would we set our eyes on the knowledge that God has an eternal purpose in the good and difficult times of our lives. The Bible speaks a lot about heavenly rewards for the saints that will last forever; whereas, earthly rewards are temporal. When you think about it, Jesus is the greatest reward set before us. He is our inheritance and our joy.

11. These are just a few things that your group members may bring up (some may not be found in this chapter): Asking God for an eternal perspective on our life's circumstances; Knowing God is with us always and will never leave or forsake us in any way; Knowing that God has an eternal purpose in everything that happens whether we understand it or not, i.e. Joseph's story and Joseph's declaration of Genesis 50:20; Knowing God loves us and has proven His love (He died for us) and that He has good plans for us; Knowing that our trials are working steadfastness and Christ's image in us; Knowing God is unchangeable and not like humans who lie, deceive and change their minds – therefore, we can trust Him. Knowing Christ promises to bring us through and we have His strength, power and wisdom available to us; Knowing we have eternal rewards that will last forever and whatever we gain or endure on earth is temporal; Knowing God is in control.

12. Be joyful. It is a command. Decide to rejoice. Pray and give thanks in all circumstances. Verse 9 of John 15 tells us to abide in His love. We need to stay connected to Christ, the vine at all times. Maintain a consistent relationship with Christ, spending time with Him daily in prayer and reading His Word. His presence in our lives on a consistent basis allows His life to flow into and through ours. It brings us the strength and wisdom we need so that we do not fall under the weight of despair during trying times nor do we fall under the deception of riches or success during good times. Living life with Christ keeps us steady and enables us to endure whatever comes our way. Our joy in Him can be constant as we focus on God and eternal things.

Chapter Seven - Leader's Guide

1. We will have tribulation while journeying on the earth with a promise that He will bring us through (He has overcome the world), and as we abide in Him, we can have peace.

2. Christ has overcome the world and His victory is ours. God promises to work all of our trials and good times alike to our (those who are in Christ) good according to His purpose and plan. Also see Jeremiah 29:11.

3. His righteous behavior was seen in his humility towards God. Instead of, "Why me, Lord?" his attitude was basically one of, "Why not me, Lord?"

4. Personal reflection outside of group. Comment for group: If anything or anyone carries our heart more than Christ, we will have unrealistic expectations of them. They cannot take the place in our lives that belongs only to God. Only He is the same yesterday, today and forever. Therefore, we are sure to be disappointed at times and perhaps even fall into depression if our primary focus is anything but Him.

5. Personal reflection. Perhaps determine the areas of your life that you have not yet surrendered to Him, trusting Him with it, repenting of sitting on the throne that belongs to Him. He has purchased you and the throne of your heart is to be His. If Jesus is truly to be one's Lord, He must be kept first in the allocation of one's time and resources. Many find this is an area where they need to make changes.

6. Trials are a result of the fall and we all have varying kinds while on earth. We put our faith in God and not in our circumstances, our faith or a particular answer to our prayers. Whatever His answer is to our prayers, we accept and ask for His strength to endure until He delivers us. The Apostle Paul talks of having a "thorn in his flesh" and that he sought God to remove it. God responded, "My grace is sufficient for you." You may want to read the account in 2 Corinthians 12:7-10.

7. No. Again, our faith is seen in accepting God's rule in our lives. His ways are higher than our ways so our finite minds do not always understand; but, we can still trust Him because He has proven who He is in our lives, through Christ. Faith is seen most when prayers are not answered the way we desire because that is when we discover if our faith is really in God as Lord of our lives or is it in ourselves and what we think is best for us and those around us. If He is the object of our faith, we trust His answer has an eternal purpose for us and perhaps others as well. Consider the story of Job. His story of suffering and deliverance has comforted and encouraged thousands of people over the years.

Perhaps that was God's purpose for it; yet, Job never knew. Perhaps he has a special reward in heaven for eternity. Ultimately, we should pray and accept *"Your Kingdom come and your will be done on earth as it is in heaven."*

8. Unbelief is the biggest reason for our need to control. We don't trust that God will do what is best so we need to handle it. If we believe God is who He says He is and will do what he says He will do, we can release control. We can spend time in the Word and prayer to increase in our knowledge of God and the power of salvation in Christ. Sometimes our need to control is a result of believing that if we fail, we are worthy of punishment. We do not understand fully the doctrine of propitiation found in 1 John 4:9-11. We don't understand that Christ satisfied God's wrath by His death on the cross and that no matter if we fail or not in any of our life's endeavors, we are still loved tremendously, accepted by the One who really matters. When we get this truth into our belief system, our fear of failure decreases and we are able to release control. We can ask God to help us receive His truth and be set free.

9. God's goal for His children is holiness – He desires that we reflect the image of His only begotten son, Jesus Christ. God also knows that genuine happiness is a by-product of holiness. You cannot be truly happy without moving towards Christ and godly living.

10. Without a knowledge of God and His ways, you will not recognize Him in the affairs of life nor will you have faith in Him. Without faith in Him, you will always be second guessing God's responses to your life which will rob your peace.

11. God has sovereign authority and power over our lives. There should be personal responses as to how this truth makes group members feel. If they understand that God loves them so greatly, if they really grasp the truth of the cross, then they can know that His authority and power over our lives is a wonderful thing even beyond our comprehension. Be sure to maintain an atmosphere of acceptance, however, should some members have negative feelings about this truth. Remember, God reveals truths to each of us and perfects each of us in His own timing.

12. As leader of the group, you should read these chapters and pick out a couple of things to share from each. Lead a discussion on what it really means to commit to Christ and encourage the group to prepare themselves to be able to stand even should persecution come to us in our land, just for being a Christian.

Chapter Eight - Leader's Guide

1. This question is designed for personal reflection. You could ask this as a general question in the group by asking how people in general tend to put unrealistic expectations on the different groups in the question, as well as with co-workers in the workplace, and how it might affect the one who is doing so, as well as the recipient of such expectation.

2. This is another personal reflection question. However, it is possible to discuss the attributes of a bondservant to Christ. Please review pages 104 through 106 for my discussion on this topic.

3. Serving others, demands that we lay down our pride and our rights and deliberately choose to identify and meet a need we see in another. Since our focus is not on ourselves and what we want or need, it is quite difficult for whatever they do to get under our skin, offend us and cause strife. Their defensive mechanisms, caused many times from their insecurity, jealousy and concern that you may desire, for example, to take something from them – perhaps their position or power – are often dismantled as they realize you desire nothing from them, but only desire to give and see them succeed and be happy.

   There are times, that the person you are trying to serve, may not receive your servant heart. But, I believe more times than not, others' hearts are softened when they see a humble servant. They begin to feel less threatened and are able to just relax.

4. This question is intended for inner reflection as to what each person can do in their own personal life to partner with God in this process. Of course, we all must surrender to the process if we are to make any progress at all.

5. See the last paragraph of page 107 and be sure to read the account in Matthew 18:23-35. If time permits, you may want to read this Scripture together in your group meeting. Only God is worthy to judge another, so we must forgive others no matter how much they have hurt us. God did not hold our sin against Him, against us; so, how can we possibly hold another responsible for their sin against us. We are empowered to forgive through our relationship with Christ. When we don't, we effectually find ourselves in a prison without bars, tortured by sleeplessness, anger and bitterness (the torturers). This condition can digress to the point that it affects every area of one's life.

6. Here are a few of the answers found in this passage: Vs9-By living according to God's Word. Vs10-By seeking God (abide in Christ). You can't refrain from sin apart from God. Vs11-Hiding God's Word in our hearts (memorize

Scripture). Vs13- Speaking the Word. Vs14-Rejoicing. Vs15-Meditating on Scripture. Vs16-Delighting in the Word versus neglecting it. Vs17-Asking for God's help to obey. Vs21-Remaining humble. God sees others from the perspective of who they *can* be. When we see others through His eyes, it affects everything in our dealings with them.

7. Personal reflection, optional for group discussion.

8. Personal reflection, optional for group discussion.

9. This is also a personal reflection question; however, your members could discuss, as a group, some general acts of kindness. You may want to think of some acts of kindness that you can do for those in your daily lives, including towards those who are not in a position to benefit you in any way, apart from the inward joy experienced through the act of giving.

10. Be devoted to them as a brother/(sister). Honor them. Keep your zeal and serve the Lord (note: this is a good witness to others). Be joyful. Be patient. Be faithful in prayer. Share with those in need. Be hospitable. Bless those who persecute you. Rejoice with others in every circumstance. Live in harmony. Be humble towards all no matter their position in life. Do not be conceited. Be careful to do what is right. Don't pay evil for evil. Live at peace with others, as far as it depends on you. Do not take revenge.

Chapter Nine - Leader's Guide

1. When we look to them as our source for whatever it is we need to include satisfaction.

2. Personal reflection question for each member to determine what needs changed in their own heart and lifestyle so that they can spend more time with Christ, putting Him as their first priority in life.

3. You will love one and hate the other or be devoted to one and despise the other (Matthew 6:24).

4. We have not yet received all the benefits of salvation. We are not perfect. However, that should not prevent us from leaving the past behind and pressing forward each day to the goal of life in glory. We know that one day our salvation will be made complete in Christ, who has called us heavenward.

5. A cluttered heart has divided devotions. An uncluttered heart is loyal to God above all else.

6. On Christ and our citizenship in heaven. If we will devote ourselves to reading Scripture, and sharing the gospel and Christ with others, it will help us keep our focus on Him and heaven. The importance of witnessing cannot be overly stressed for its importance to our success to maintain our focus on Christ while we live in an ungodly world, surrounded and tempted by all kinds of distractions. Unlike a dead sea, we are to be like a river where water flows in and out.

7. Our life should be defined by our relationship to Christ. Becoming like Him should be our goal. While on the journey, we realize that our worth has already been determined. The ultimate price was paid for us, the life of God. This frees us from searching for value in people, positions and acquisition of material things. God is the one who makes us who we are for His purposes on earth. He has made us rich in spiritual things and has given us high status as His child and as a citizen of the Kingdom of God.

8. A person who is double-minded seeks mutually exclusive and *conflicting* goals. Therefore, when you have this mind, you are unable to believe and have faith to receive either goal.

9. Pay close attention to what God has said in Scripture and never let it leave our hearts.

10. Philippians answers this question straight-forwardly. You may want to ask the members of your group to consider whether this thought for their life brings them satisfaction.

Chapter Ten - Leader's Guide

1. Personal testimony to share with group. Choose one volunteer to share a short testimony. Again, you will need to give a time limit determined by the number of questions you desire to discuss in the meeting.

2. If time permits, choose a volunteer to share. You could save this question for the end of the session.

3. Oftentimes, we don't understand why God would let us be in the struggle, in the first place. We need to accept that God is sovereign and that He loves us. We need to accept that we cannot understand the infinite mind of God with our limited, finite minds no more than a three-year-old understands why we do the things we do, including our discipline of their inappropriate behavior.

4. Allow some group discussion for this question. Share some encouraging words from the chapter or as God gives them to you, concerning the acceptance of this truth.

5. Think about your personal answer to this question. Ask group members who would like to share before sharing yourself.

6. Accepting by faith, the love of God, builds confidence in God and in trusting Him with our lives. Experiencing God's love also dispels fear of punishment and rejection which allows us to walk in the liberty Christ came to give us (freedom of fear of failure, rejection, shame and the need to be perfect). Receiving His love into our life, brings satisfaction.

7. Allow a few group members to share and/or share yourself.

8. Allow a few group members to share and/or share yourself.

9. You will always second guess God's responses to your life's circumstances. It is impossible to experience *real* satisfaction without having confidence in God.

10. You may want to use your Bible concordance or an online service such as Biblegateway.com to look up some Scriptures where these various attributes are spoken of concerning God. Remember that immutability speaks of God's unchangeableness. His omniscience speaks of Him being all-knowledgeable. Omnipotence speaks of God possessing all-power and God's omnipresence speaks of God's presence – He is everywhere present all at the same time. And, God IS love and has shown us what love is. Help the group members to relate these powerful truths to their lives.

Chapter Eleven - Leader's Guide

1. Some answers might be: I feel ashamed. Life is hopeless – John 3:3-6 speaks of a believer's regeneration; I need to please people or a certain person and I am fearful of criticism – Colossians 1:21-22 speaks of our reconciliation with God; When I fail, I fear punishment so I tend to avoid failure – 1 John 4:9-11; I tend to set standards of perfectionism for myself and when I fail to meet them, I am anxious and angry – 1 John 4:9-11 speaks of the doctrine of propitiation. Christ satisfied God's wrath by His death. God has a deep love for those who belong to Christ.

2. Our spirits are born again; however, our minds are not yet changed. And, there is no escape from our carnality but by the abiding presence of the Holy Spirit (Romans 7:19-20). As we press forward COMMITTED to godliness, the law of the Spirit then assures us victory (Romans 8:2). We all have strongholds and habit patterns embedded in our physical minds. We need to follow Romans 12:2 instructions and partner with the Holy Spirit in renewing our minds to line up with God's mind.

3. Repent, receive God's cleansing and forgiveness and move forward with God, free of guilt and condemnation.

4. Be careful not to confuse our value with our actions. Our value is determined by the price paid for us – the life of Christ. Our actions are not always in line with who we are as a new creation in Christ. That character is still being worked out in us as we surrender to the work of the Holy Spirit. As we focus on Christ and who He calls us to be, we will begin to increasingly walk in the liberty and holiness of Christ and one day, when we are face to face with Him, we will be perfected.

5. When people feel hopeless, believing they are unable to change, they are trapped with feelings of shame, inferiority and many times it causes them to withdraw from others. Believers need to understand and accept the truths in Scripture that declare who they are as a new creation in Christ. The doctrine of regeneration declares that the old life is gone and a new life has begun. As they renew their minds and belief system to this, they will begin to walk in it.

6. Issues of rejection can often times be healed when one believes the doctrine of reconciliation which declares that they are forgiven and totally accepted by God, and that He desires an intimate relationship with them. If God is for us, who can be against us?

7. Realize that Christ has already determined your worth. You are valuable just as you are (sin and all) and do not need to do anything or be anything more to be loved and accepted by God. What you do will not make God love or accept you any more or any less. However, it can affect your rewards; and it can affect your fellowship with God since sin causes us to hide from God.

8. There could be several answers given for this question. One answer is that we underestimate our value without knowing who we are in Christ. With that underestimation, we are dissatisfied with who we are.

9. When we don't agree with God in anything, God calls it unbelief so it is sin. He has called us to repent and to ask Him to help us accept His truth, and renew our minds accordingly. He helps us as He is dwelling in us at all times. As we make a decision to follow Him; and we desire to have a belief system that lines up with truth, He will begin to illuminate truth to us. Scripture says that the secret of the Lord is with those who fear Him and to them He reveals His covenant (Psalm 25:14). Thus, it is safe to say our attitude towards God is important.

10. Self-esteem and God-esteem. Self-esteem is faith in what *I* can do and God esteem is having faith in what *I can do with God's life living through me* (or joined with mine). The Lord is my shepherd and I shall not want (Psalm 23).

Paul said, I can do all things in the strength of Christ (Philippians 4:13). Also, see 2 Cor. 12:9.

11. We are created to fulfill a purpose. Every human being chosen by God has an eternal purpose. There is no purpose as great as to glorify God with one's life. As we do this, we are the most satisfied.

Chapter Twelve - Leader's Guide

1. See "Things to Remember" section.

2. All of creation groans as it waits for redemption.

3. We groan and are burdened waiting for what is mortal, with its weakness and imperfections, to be swallowed by life. Meanwhile, we have the Spirit as a deposit to guarantee what is to come.

4. No death, mourning, crying or pain. No longer will there be any effects of the curse.

5. God's presence satisfies. His love satisfies. He is with us all of the time in spirit; yet, we hunger to be with Him in our immortal state (2 Corinthians 5:6). We are constantly distracted by the worldly responsibilities and challenges that surround us, as well as the sin that still dwells in our bodies as we are still in the process of sanctification. However, when we meet Christ face to face, He will complete His work of perfecting us, and we will experience the fullness of His presence in our lives without end. We will be one with Him.

6. The Kingdom of God and His righteousness.

7. Ask someone to read these Scriptures and help the group turn this into a prayer.

8. This is a question to stimulate individual responses.

9. This is a question for personal responses.

10. Discuss with the group how you may be able to hold one another accountable in your pursuit of God, His Kingdom and righteousness so that you may maintain satisfaction while waiting to be with the Lord.

   You may want to ask the group if they would like to do the study on godliness, with the second book in my Abundant Living Package: *Experience Godliness God's Way*. This book together with the study you just completed was influenced by the Scripture: *Godliness with contentment is great gain* (1 Timothy 6:6).

Endnotes ———————————————————

[1] *The American Heritage College Dictionary*, Third Edition, Copyright 1993 by Houghton Mifflin Company, Boston MA, page 419.

[2] Warren Wiersbe, *Be Satisfied* (Colorado Springs, CO, Cook Communications 2005), 11.

[3] Warren Wiersbe, *Be Satisfied* (Colorado Springs, CO, Cook Communications 2005), 19.

[4] Dr. Bruce Demarest, *Satisfy Your Soul* (Colorado Springs, CO Navpress 1999), 50.

[5] Dr. Bruce Demarest, *Satisfy Your Soul* (Colorado Springs, CO Navpress 1999), 285.

[6] *Blue Letter Bible.* "Dictionary and Word Search for 'perissos' (Strong's 4053)." Blue Letter Bible. 1996-2002. 27 Jul 2006. http://www.blueletterbible.org.

[7] Carnegie, *How To Stop Worrying and Start Living* (New York: Simon and Schuster, 1948), 19 & 96.

[8] William J. Bouwsma, John Calvin, *A Sixteenth-Century Portrait* (New York: Oxford University Press, 1988), 37.

[9] Robert J. Morgan, *Nelson's Complete Book of Stories, Illustrations, & Quotes* (Nashville, TN: 2003), Copyright © by Robert J. Morgan. All rights reserved, 801.

[10] Matthew Henry's *Concise Commentary on the Bible*, Matthew Chapter 6, Trust in God commended., www.biblegateway.com, Public Domain.

[11] Matthew Henry's *Concise Commentary on the Bible*, Ephesians Chapter 6, All Christians are to put on spiritual armour against the enemies of their souls., www.biblegateway.com, Public Domain.

[12] Ibid.

[13] Robert J. Morgan, *Nelson's Complete Book of Stories, Illustrations, & Quotes* (Nashville, TN: 2003), Copyright © by Robert J. Morgan. All rights reserved, 803-804.

[14] *The American Heritage® Dictionary of the English Language*, Fourth Edition Copyright © 2000 by Houghton Mifflin Company. Published by Houghton Mifflin Company. All rights reserved.

[15] Holman Bible Publishers (Nashville, TN web: www.broadmanholman.com). Copyright © 1991 Holman Bible Publishers. All rights reserved. International copyright secured.

[16] With thanks to Michael Fletcher, whose sermon inspired these thoughts.

[17] *New Spirit-Filled Life Bible*, Copyright © 2002 by Thomas Nelson, Inc. All rights reserved, 792.

[18] Elmer L. Towns, *My Father's Names* (Ventura, CA: Regal Books 1991). Names of God and descriptions were compiled from this book.

[19] Wayne Grudem, *Bible Doctrine: "Essential Teachings of the Christian Faith"* (Grand Rapids, MI: Zondervan 1999, 88.

[20] Robert McGee, *In Search of Significance* (Nashville, TN: W Publishing Group, Div of Thomas Nelson 2003).

[21] Ibid.

[22] *New Spirit- Filled Life Bible*, Commentary on Romans 6:6, (Nashville, TN: Thomas Nelson, Inc. Copyright ©2002). All rights reserved, 1558.

[23] Ibid.

[24] *Westminster Catechism*, Shorter Version, Question 1, www.reformed.org/documents/ WSC.

[25] The gospel rendering was taken from Booklet E083G of *Evangelism Explosion Int'l*

Other Books by Sarah

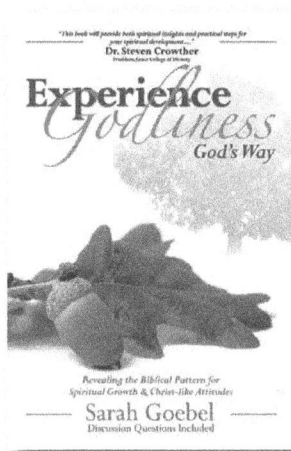

A Look at God's Pattern for Spiritual Growth - Refreshing and Doable!

You can learn how to enjoy God on your journey to Christ-likeness. But, first, you must begin the pursuit, or the life Christ has made available this side of heaven could be forfeited. Yet, to progress toward godliness requires that one knows what God's idea of perfection really is. In *Experience Godliness God's Way*, you will discover the surprising answer while learning how to rest in the process.

This interactive, practical study of the spiritual disciplines (God's tools for changing us from glory to glory) is a refreshing way to discover...

- The freedom and enjoyment that comes from living on purpose for godly transformation.
- The importance and power of the spiritual disciplines
- How the spiritual disciplines will help you grow in the likeness of Christ
- How the spiritual disciplines are not to be a form of bondage but an opportunity for genuine freedom to enjoy God and the life He desires for you.

Spiritual formation is a goal, not born out of duty, but out of love. If you are ready to acknowledge your need and desire for spiritual formation, you will benefit from this short, interactive study.

This study is especially designed for the busy Christian who desires a group study without homework. Group members work through the material together.

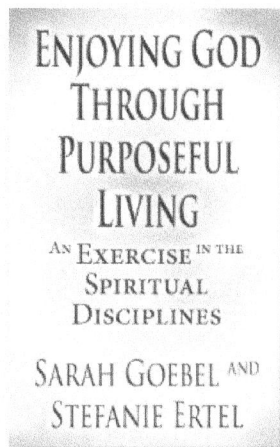

I would love to hear from you!

Please take a minute or two to drop me a line at:
My Blog: www.BlogwithSarah.com
Facebook: www.facebook.com/CoachSarah
Email: Sarah@sarahgoebel.com

Visit my website at:

www.SarahGoebel.com

(Be sure to register for my FREE devotionals and newsletters)

Media Site: www.sermon.net/dham

Looking for a life coach?

Let me help you get to where you want to go!
Together we will:
DISCOVER OPTIONS, IMPLEMENT STRATEGIES
& NAVIGATE CHANGES FOR SUCCESS!
Find out More At: www.sarahgoebel.com

Please let me know how God used this book in your life.
IF YOU SAID THE SALVATION PRAYER
with a sincere heart, while reading this book,
"Congratulations & Welcome to the Family!"
Let me know, and I will have a free gift for you.

Financial support may be given through
Declaring His Answer Ministries,
the 501c3 covering for
Sarah Goebel & Family Secrets Ministry.
This can be done online at:
www.SarahGoebel.com

The On Assignment Publishing Vision

Challenging Christian writers
to complete the assignment
God has put on their hearts

Providing a vehicle for Christian writers to fulfill their
assignment and to proclaim Christ and principles of the
Christian faith through fiction and non-fiction books.

Challenging readers and authors to work
faith principles out in their lives, to stand firm
in the faith and to enjoy God in the process.

May Christ be glorified.

On Assignment
PUBLISHING
Our Assignment is to Help You Complete Yours

www.OnAssignmentPublishing.com

www.ingramcontent.com/pod-product-compliance
Lightning Source LLC
Chambersburg PA
CBHW031955040426
42448CB00006B/372